Gradle for Android

Automate the build process for your Android
projects with Gradle

Kevin Pelgrims

PUBLISHING

BIRMINGHAM - MUMBAI

Gradle for Android

First published: July 2015

Production reference: 1140715

Published by Packt Publishing Ltd.
Livery Place
35 Livery Street
Birmingham B3 2PB, UK.

ISBN 978-1-78398-682-8

www.packtpub.com

Credits

Author

Kevin Pelgrims

Reviewers

Peter Friese

Jonathan H. Kau

Takuya Miyamoto

Marco A. Rodriguez-Suarez

Felix Schulze

Hugo Visser

Commissioning Editor

Amarabha Banerjee

Acquisition Editor

Nikhil Karkal

Content Development Editor

Prachi Bisht

Technical Editor

Pankaj Kadam

Copy Editors

Puja Lalwani

Laxmi Subramanian

Project Coordinator

Shipra Chawhan

Proofreader

Safis Editing

Indexer

Tejal Soni

Production Coordinator

Manu Joseph

Cover Work

Manu Joseph

About the Author

Kevin Pelgrims started his career as a .NET developer in Belgium. After some years working on Windows and web development for corporate clients, he moved to Copenhagen to become part of its start-up community. There, he began working on mobile platforms, and within a year, he was the lead developer of several Android and Windows Phone apps. Kevin is also a regular speaker at the Android developers group in Copenhagen. He maintains multiple Android apps in his spare time and likes to experiment with server-side technology. When he is not busy writing code, he is most likely playing the guitar with his wife and their cat.

To follow what Kevin is up to, you can take a look at his blog at `http://www.kevinpelgrims.com` or follow him on Twitter at @kevinpelgrims.

I could not have written this book without the support of my brilliant wife, Louise. Not only did she put up with me spending entire evenings and weekends with my computer, she also proofread the entire book, improving the language and the grammar.

I would like to thank Packt Publishing for giving me the opportunity to write this book, especially Nikhil Karkal and Prachi Bisht, for believing in me and guiding me throughout the process. I appreciate the help of my friend Koen Metsu, whose comments helped in making sure that the explanations and examples are easy to understand. Thanks to Anders Bo Pedersen and Emanuele Zattin for coming up with several improvements.

I also want to thank the reviewers: Hugo Visser, Peter Friese, Felix Schulze, Takuya Miyamoto, Jonathan H. Kau, and Marco Rodriguez-Suarez. Their input has significantly improved the content of this book. Last but not least, special thanks to our cat, Jigsaw, who encouraged me to stay focused and keep going, by sitting on my lap so I couldn't get up.

About the Reviewers

Peter Friese works as a developer advocate at Google in the Developer Relations team in London, UK. He is a regular open source contributor, blogger, and public speaker. He is on Twitter at @peterfriese and on Google+ at +PeterFriese. You can find his blog at http://www.peterfriese.de.

Jonathan H. Kau is an experienced Android developer, having published several standalone applications to Google Play and worked on numerous hackathon projects leveraging Android.

In the past, he has worked on the mobile team at Yelp and as a contractor for Propeller Labs. Jonathan is currently working in the engineering team at Shyp, both on the Android application and the corresponding backend API.

> I'd like to thank Packt Publishing for giving me the opportunity to review this educational book that will hopefully simplify the use of Gradle for many developers.

Takuya Miyamoto is a full-stack developer with 6 years of experience in designing, implementing, and maintaining various types of web services and APIs such as e-commerce and SNS. He also has some experience as an Android developer. He has worked as a senior engineer in an enterprise, as a lead engineer in start-ups, and is currently working as an individual developer.

Marco A. Rodriguez-Suarez is the head of mobile at Snapwire, a collaborative platform and marketplace that connects photographers with brands and businesses around the world. Prior to that, he worked in mobile consulting on diverse projects, ranging from topics such as video streaming to game emulation. He has been working with Android since the release of the first public device in 2008 and has been hooked on mobile development ever since. He is passionate about build systems and has extensive experience with Gradle, Maven, and Ant. Marco received his master's degree in electrical engineering from the University of California at Santa Barbara.

Felix Schulze is leading the mobile software development department at AutoScout24 and is responsible for the Android and iOS development. He also gives a lot of talks about continuous integration in app development and contributes to open source tools. His Twitter handle is `@x2on`; you can also check out his website at `www.felixschulze.de`.

Hugo Visser has many years of experience as a software engineer, ranging from server-side to desktop and from web to mobile. Since the original announcement, he has closely followed the development of the Android platform, which resulted in his first app in 2009, *Rainy Days*, which has since been downloaded over 1,000,000 times worldwide.

He runs his own company, Little Robots, which focuses on apps and other clever uses of the Android platform. He has been named the Google Developer Expert for Android by Google and is an organizer of The Dutch Android User Group, which is a community in the Netherlands where Android professionals can meet and share knowledge with each other during monthly meetings.

www.PacktPub.com

Support files, eBooks, discount offers, and more

For support files and downloads related to your book, please visit www.PacktPub.com.

Did you know that Packt offers eBook versions of every book published, with PDF and ePub files available? You can upgrade to the eBook version at www.PacktPub.com and as a print book customer, you are entitled to a discount on the eBook copy. Get in touch with us at service@packtpub.com for more details.

At www.PacktPub.com, you can also read a collection of free technical articles, sign up for a range of free newsletters and receive exclusive discounts and offers on Packt books and eBooks.

https://www2.packtpub.com/books/subscription/packtlib

Do you need instant solutions to your IT questions? PacktLib is Packt's online digital book library. Here, you can search, access, and read Packt's entire library of books.

Why subscribe?

- Fully searchable across every book published by Packt
- Copy and paste, print, and bookmark content
- On demand and accessible via a web browser

Free access for Packt account holders

If you have an account with Packt at www.PacktPub.com, you can use this to access PacktLib today and view 9 entirely free books. Simply use your login credentials for immediate access.

Table of Contents

Preface   **vii**

Chapter 1: Getting Started with Gradle and Android Studio   **1**
  Android Studio   **2**
    Staying up to date   3
  Understanding Gradle basics   **3**
    Projects and tasks   4
    The build lifecycle   4
    The build configuration file   4
  Creating a new project   **7**
  Getting started with the Gradle Wrapper   **10**
    Getting the Gradle Wrapper   10
    Running basic build tasks   12
  Migrating from Eclipse   **13**
    Using the import wizard   14
    Migrating manually   15
      Keeping the old project structure   15
      Converting to the new project structure   17
      Migrating libraries   18
  Summary   **18**

Chapter 2: Basic Build Customization   **19**
  Understanding the Gradle files   **19**
    The settings file   20
    The top-level build file   20
    The module build file   21
      Plugin   22
      Android   22
      Dependencies   24

Getting started with tasks	**24**
Base tasks	24
Android tasks	25
Inside Android Studio	26
Customizing the build	**28**
Manipulating manifest entries	29
Inside Android Studio	29
BuildConfig and resources	30
Project-wide settings	31
Project properties	32
Default tasks	33
Summary	**33**
Chapter 3: Managing Dependencies	**35**
Repositories	**35**
Preconfigured repositories	37
Remote repositories	37
Local repositories	38
Local dependencies	**39**
File dependencies	39
Native libraries	40
Library projects	41
Creating and using library project modules	41
Using .aar files	42
Dependency concepts	**42**
Configurations	42
Semantic versioning	43
Dynamic versions	44
Inside Android Studio	**44**
Summary	**46**
Chapter 4: Creating Build Variants	**47**
Build types	**48**
Creating build types	48
Source sets	50
Dependencies	52
Product flavors	**52**
Creating product flavors	52
Source sets	53
Multiflavor variants	53
Build variants	**54**
Tasks	55

Source sets	56
Resource and manifest merging	56
Creating build variants	57
Variant filters	58
Signing configurations	**59**
Summary	**61**
Chapter 5: Managing Multimodule Builds	**63**
The anatomy of a multimodule build	**64**
The build lifecycle revisited	65
Module tasks	66
Adding modules to a project	**67**
Adding a Java library	68
Adding an Android library	68
Integrating Android Wear	69
Using Google App Engine	70
Analyzing the build file	71
Using the backend in an app	72
Custom tasks	73
Tips and best practices	**73**
Running module tasks from Android Studio	74
Speeding up multimodule builds	74
Module coupling	75
Summary	**76**
Chapter 6: Running Tests	**77**
Unit tests	**77**
JUnit	78
Robolectric	81
Functional tests	**82**
Espresso	82
Test coverage	**86**
Jacoco	87
Summary	**88**
Chapter 7: Creating Tasks and Plugins	**89**
Understanding Groovy	**89**
Introduction	90
Classes and members	91
Methods	92
Closures	93
Collections	93
Groovy in Gradle	94

Getting started with tasks	**95**
Defining tasks	95
Anatomy of a task	98
Using a task to simplify the release process	100
Hooking into the Android plugin	**104**
Automatically renaming APKs	104
Dynamically creating new tasks	105
Creating your own plugins	**107**
Creating a simple plugin	107
Distributing plugins	108
Using a custom plugin	111
Summary	**111**
Chapter 8: Setting Up Continuous Integration	**113**
Jenkins	**114**
Setting up Jenkins	114
Configuring the build	115
TeamCity	**117**
Setting up TeamCity	118
Configuring the build	118
Travis CI	**119**
Configuring the build	119
Further automation	**122**
The SDK manager plugin	122
Running tests	122
Continuous deployment	123
Beta distribution	125
Summary	**126**
Chapter 9: Advanced Build Customization	**127**
Reducing the APK file size	**127**
ProGuard	128
Shrinking resources	129
Automatic shrinking	129
Manual shrinking	130
Speeding up builds	**131**
Gradle properties	131
Android Studio	133
Profiling	134
Jack and Jill	135
Ignoring Lint	**136**

Using Ant from Gradle	**136**
Running Ant tasks from Gradle	136
Importing an entire Ant script	137
Properties	139
Advanced app deployment	**139**
Split APK	139
Summary	**141**
Index	**143**

Preface

The build process for an Android app is an incredibly complex procedure that involves many tools. To begin with, all the resource files are compiled and referenced in a R.java file, before the Java code is compiled and then converted to Dalvik bytecode by the dex tool. These files are then packaged into an APK file, and that APK file is signed with a debug or release key, before the app can finally be installed onto a device.

Going through all these steps manually would be a tedious and time-consuming undertaking. Luckily, the Android Tools team has continued to provide developers with tools that take care of the entire process, and in 2013, they introduced Gradle as the new preferred build system for Android apps. Gradle is designed in a way that makes it easy to extend builds and plug into the existing build processes. It provides a Groovy-like DSL to declare builds and create tasks, and makes dependency management easy. Additionally, it is completely free and open source.

By now, most Android developers have switched to Gradle, but many do not know how to make the best of it, and are unaware of what can be achieved with just a few lines of code. This book aims to help those developers, and turn them into Gradle power users. Starting with the basics of Gradle in an Android context, this book goes on to cover dependencies, build variants, testing, creating tasks, and more.

What this book covers

Chapter 1, *Getting Started with Gradle and Android Studio*, explains why Gradle is useful, how to get started with Android Studio, and what the Gradle Wrapper is.

Chapter 2, *Basic Build Customization*, goes into detail about the Gradle build files and tasks, and shows how to do simple customizations to the build process.

Chapter 3, *Managing Dependencies*, shows how to use dependencies, both local and remote ones, and explains dependency-related concepts.

Chapter 4, Creating Build Variants, introduces build types and product flavors, explains what the difference between them is, and shows how to use signing configurations.

Chapter 5, Managing Multimodule Builds, explains how to manage app, library, and test modules, and mentions how to integrate them into the build.

Chapter 6, Running Tests, introduces several testing frameworks for unit tests and functional tests, how to automate testing and how to get test coverage reports.

Chapter 7, Creating Tasks and Plugins, explains the basics of Groovy, and shows how to create custom tasks and how to hook them into the Android build process. This chapter also explains how to create a reusable plugin.

Chapter 8, Setting Up Continuous Integration, provides guidance on automating builds using the most commonly used CI systems.

Chapter 9, Advanced Build Customization, shows some tips and tricks to shrink APKs, speed up the build process, and split up APKs based on density or platform.

What you need for this book

To follow all the examples, you will need to have access to a computer with Microsoft Windows, Mac OS X, or Linux. You will also need to have the Java Development Kit installed, and it is recommended that you install Android Studio, as it is mentioned in most chapters.

Who this book is for

This book is for Android developers who want to get a better understanding of the build system and become masters of the build process. Throughout the book, we will go from the basics of Gradle, to creating custom tasks and plugins, and automating multiple parts of the build process. You are assumed to be familiar with developing for the Android platform.

Conventions

In this book, you will find a number of text styles that distinguish between different kinds of information. Here are some examples of these styles and an explanation of their meaning.

Code words in text, database table names, folder names, filenames, file extensions, pathnames, dummy URLs, user input, and Twitter handles are shown as follows: "Every `build.gradle` file represents a project."

A block of code is set as follows:

```
buildscript {
    repositories {
        jcenter()
    }
    dependencies {
        classpath 'com.android.tools.build:gradle:1.2.3'
    }
}
```

Any command-line input or output is written as follows:

```
$ gradlew tasks
```

New terms and **important words** are shown in bold. Words that you see on the screen, for example, in menus or dialog boxes, appear in the text like this: "You can start a new project in Android Studio by clicking on **Start a new Android Studio project** on the start screen."

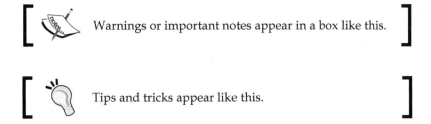

Warnings or important notes appear in a box like this.

Tips and tricks appear like this.

Reader feedback

Feedback from our readers is always welcome. Let us know what you think about this book—what you liked or disliked. Reader feedback is important for us as it helps us develop titles that you will really get the most out of.

To send us general feedback, simply e-mail feedback@packtpub.com, and mention the book's title in the subject of your message.

If there is a topic that you have expertise in and you are interested in either writing or contributing to a book, see our author guide at www.packtpub.com/authors.

Customer support

Now that you are the proud owner of a Packt book, we have a number of things to help you to get the most from your purchase.

Downloading the example code

You can download the example code files from your account at `http://www.packtpub.com` for all the Packt Publishing books you have purchased. If you purchased this book elsewhere, you can visit `http://www.packtpub.com/support` and register to have the files e-mailed directly to you.

Errata

Although we have taken every care to ensure the accuracy of our content, mistakes do happen. If you find a mistake in one of our books—maybe a mistake in the text or the code—we would be grateful if you could report this to us. By doing so, you can save other readers from frustration and help us improve subsequent versions of this book. If you find any errata, please report them by visiting `http://www.packtpub.com/submit-errata`, selecting your book, clicking on the **Errata Submission Form** link, and entering the details of your errata. Once your errata are verified, your submission will be accepted and the errata will be uploaded to our website or added to any list of existing errata under the Errata section of that title.

To view the previously submitted errata, go to `https://www.packtpub.com/books/content/support` and enter the name of the book in the search field. The required information will appear under the **Errata** section.

Piracy

Piracy of copyrighted material on the Internet is an ongoing problem across all media. At Packt, we take the protection of our copyright and licenses very seriously. If you come across any illegal copies of our works in any form on the Internet, please provide us with the location address or website name immediately so that we can pursue a remedy.

Please contact us at `copyright@packtpub.com` with a link to the suspected pirated material.

We appreciate your help in protecting our authors and our ability to bring you valuable content.

Questions

If you have a problem with any aspect of this book, you can contact us at
questions@packtpub.com, and we will do our best to address the problem.

1
Getting Started with Gradle and Android Studio

When Google introduced Gradle and Android Studio, they had some goals in mind. They wanted to make it easier to reuse code, create build variants, and configure and customize the build process. On top of that, they wanted good IDE integration, but without making the build system dependent on the IDE. Running Gradle from the command line or on a continuous integration server will always yield the same results as running a build from Android Studio.

We will refer to Android Studio occasionally throughout the book, because it often provides a simpler way of setting up projects, dealing with changes, and so on. If you do not have Android Studio installed yet, you can download it from the Android developer website (`http://developer.android.com/sdk/index.html`).

In this chapter, we will cover the following topics:

- Getting to know Android Studio
- Understanding Gradle basics
- Creating a new project
- Getting started with the Gradle wrapper
- Migrating from Eclipse

Android Studio

Android Studio was announced and released (as an early access preview) by Google in May 2013, alongside support for Gradle. Android Studio is based on JetBrains' IntelliJ IDEA, but is designed specifically with Android development in mind. It is available for free for Linux, Mac OS X, and Microsoft Windows.

Compared to Eclipse, Android Studio has an improved user interface designer, a better memory monitor, a nice editor for string translation, warnings for possible Android-specific issues and a lot more features aimed at Android developers. It also features a special project structure view for Android projects, besides the regular Project view and Packages view that exist in IntelliJ IDEA. This special view groups Gradle scripts, drawables, and other resources in a convenient way. As soon as the stable version 1.0 of Android Studio was released, Google retired the **Android Developer Tools (ADT)** for Eclipse and recommended all developers to switch to Android Studio. This means that Google will not provide new features for Eclipse anymore, and all IDE-related tool development is now focused on Android Studio. If you are still using Eclipse, it is time to change if you do not want to be left behind.

This screenshot shows what Android Studio looks like for a simple Android app project:

Staying up to date

There are four different update channels for Android Studio:

- Canary brings bleeding-edge updates, but might contain some bugs
- The Dev channel gets an update more or less every month
- Beta is used feature complete updates that might still contain bugs
- The Stable channel, which is the default, features thoroughly tested releases that should be bug-free

By default, Android Studio checks every time it starts if there any updates available and notifies you.

When you launch Android Studio for the first time, it starts a wizard to set up your environment and to make sure you have the latest Android SDK and the necessary Google repositories. It also gives you the option to create an **Android Virtual Device (AVD)**, so you can run apps on the emulator.

Understanding Gradle basics

In order for an Android project to be built using Gradle, you need to set up a build script. This will always be called `build.gradle`, by convention. You will notice, as we go through the basics, that Gradle favors convention over configuration and generally provides default values for settings and properties. This makes it a lot easier to get started with a lot less configuration than that found in systems such as Ant or Maven, which have been the de facto build systems for Android projects for a long time. You do not need to absolutely comply with these conventions though, as it is usually possible to override them if needed.

Gradle build scripts are not written in the traditional XML, but in a **domain-specific language (DSL)** based on Groovy, a dynamic language for the **Java Virtual Machine (JVM)**. The team behind Gradle believes that using a declarative, DSL-style approach based on a dynamic language has significant advantages over using the more procedural, free-floating style of Ant, or any XML-based approach used by many other build systems.

That does not mean you need to know Groovy to get started with your build scripts. It is easy to read, and if you already know Java, the learning curve is not that steep. If you want to start creating your own tasks and plugins (which we will talk about in later chapters), it is useful to have a deeper understanding of Groovy. However, because it is based on the JVM, it is possible to write code for your custom plugins in Java or any other JVM-based language.

Projects and tasks

The two most important concepts in Gradle are projects and tasks. Every build is made up of at least one project, and every project contains one or more tasks. Every `build.gradle` file represents a project. Tasks are then simply defined inside the build script. When initializing the build process, Gradle assembles `Project` and `Task` objects based on the build file. A `Task` object consists of a list of `Action` objects, in the order they need to be executed. An `Action` object is a block of code that is executed, similar to a method in Java.

The build lifecycle

Executing a Gradle build is, in its simplest form, just executing actions on tasks, which are dependent on other tasks. To simplify the build process, the build tools create a dynamic model of the workflow as a **Directed Acyclic Graph (DAG)**. This means all the tasks are processed one after the other and loops are not possible. Once a task has been executed, it will not be called again. Tasks without dependencies will always be run before the others. The dependency graph is generated during the configuration phase of a build. A Gradle build has three phases:

- **Initialization**: This is where the `Project` instance is created. If there are multiple modules, each with their own `build.gradle` file, multiple projects will be created.

- **Configuration**: In this phase, the build scripts are executed, creating and configuring all the tasks for every project object.

- **Execution**: This is the phase where Gradle determines which tasks should be executed. Which tasks should be executed depends on the arguments passed for starting the build and what the current directory is.

The build configuration file

In order to have Gradle build a project, there always needs to be a `build.gradle` file. A build file for Android has a few required elements:

```
buildscript {
    repositories {
        jcenter()
    }
    dependencies {
        classpath 'com.android.tools.build:gradle:1.2.3'
    }
}
```

This is where the actual build is configured. In the repositories block, the JCenter repository is configured as a source of dependencies for the build script. JCenter is a preconfigured Maven repository and requires no extra setup; Gradle has you covered. There are several repositories available straight from Gradle and it is easy to add your own, either local or remote.

The build script block also defines a dependency on Android build tools as a classpath Maven artifact. This is where the Android plugin comes from. The Android plugin provides everything needed to build and test applications. Every Android project needs to apply the Android plugin using this line:

```
apply plugin: 'com.android.application'
```

Plugins are used to extend the capabilities of a Gradle build script. Applying a plugin to a project makes it possible for the build script to define properties and use tasks that are defined in the plugin.

> If you are building a library, you need to apply `'com.android.library'` instead. You cannot use both in the same module because that would result in a build error. A module can be either an Android application or an Android library, not both.

When using the Android plugin, Android-specific conventions can be configured and tasks only applicable to Android will be generated. The Android block in the following snippet is defined by the plugin and can be configured per project:

```
android {
    compileSdkVersion 22
    buildToolsVersion "22.0.1"
}
```

This is where the Android-specific part of the build is configured. The Android plugin provides a DSL tailored to Android's needs. The only required properties are the compilation target and the build tools. The compilation target, specified by `compileSdkVersion`, is the SDK version that should be used to compile the app. It is good practice to use the latest Android API version as the compilation target.

There are plenty of customizable properties in the `build.gradle` file. We will discuss the most important properties in *Chapter 2, Basic Build Customization*, and more possibilities throughout the rest of the book.

The project structure

Compared to the old Eclipse projects, the folder structure for Android projects has changed considerably. As mentioned earlier, Gradle favors convention over configuration and this also applies to the folder structure.

This is the folder structure that Gradle expects for a simple app:

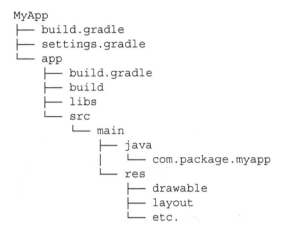

```
MyApp
├── build.gradle
├── settings.gradle
└── app
    ├── build.gradle
    ├── build
    ├── libs
    └── src
        └── main
            ├── java
            │   └── com.package.myapp
            └── res
                ├── drawable
                ├── layout
                └── etc.
```

Gradle projects usually have an extra level at the root. This makes it easier to add extra modules at a later point. All source code for the app goes into the app folder. The folder is also the name of the module by default and does not need to be named app. If you use Android Studio to create a project with both a mobile app and an Android Wear smartwatch app, for example, the modules are called application and wearable by default.

Gradle makes use of a concept called source set. The official Gradle documentation explains that a source set is *a group of source files, which are compiled and executed together*. For an Android project, main is the source set that contains all the source code and resources for the default version of the app. When you start writing tests for your Android app, you will put the source code for the tests inside a separate source set called androidTest, which only contains tests.

Here is a short overview of the most important folders of an Android app:

Directory	Content
/src/main/java	The source code for the app
/src/main/res	These are app-related resources (drawables, layouts, strings, and so on)
/libs	These are external libraries (.jar or .aar)
/build	The output of the build process

Creating a new project

You can start a new project in Android Studio by clicking on **Start a new Android Studio project** on the start screen or by navigating to **File | New Project...** in the IDE itself.

Creating a new project in Android Studio starts with a wizard that helps set everything up. The first screen is for setting up the application name and the company domain. The application name is the name that will be used as the name of the app when it is installed and is used as the toolbar title by default. The company domain is used in combination with the application name to determine the package name, which is the unique identifier for any Android app. If you prefer a different package name, you can still change it by clicking on **Edit**. You can also change the location of the project on your hard drive.

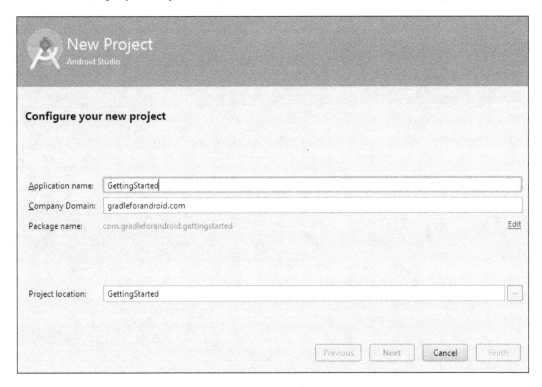

No files are generated before going through all the steps in the wizard, because the next few steps will define which files need to be created.

Android does not only run on phones and tablets, but also supports a broad range of form factors, such as TV, watches, and glasses. The next screen helps you set up all the form factors you want to target in your project. Depending on what you choose here, dependencies and build plugins are included for development. This is where you decide if you just want to make a phone and tablet app or whether you also want to include an Android TV module, an Android Wear module, or a Google Glass module. You can still add these later, but the wizard makes it easy by adding all the necessary files and configurations. This is also where you choose what version of Android you want to support. If you select an API version below 21, the Android Support Library (including the appcompat library) is automatically added as a dependency.

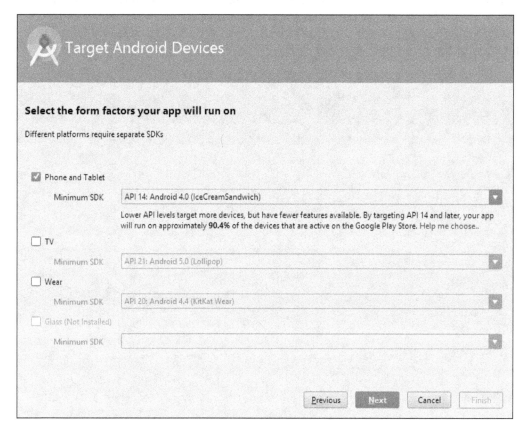

Downloading the example code

You can download the example code files from your account at http://www.packtpub.com for all the Packt Publishing books you have purchased. If you purchased this book elsewhere, you can visit http://www.packtpub.com/support and register to have the files e-mailed directly to you.

The following screen suggests adding an activity and provides a lot of options, all of which result in generated code that makes it easier to get started. If you choose to have Android Studio generate an activity for you, the next step is to enter a name for the activity class, the layout file and the menu resource, and also to give the activity a title:

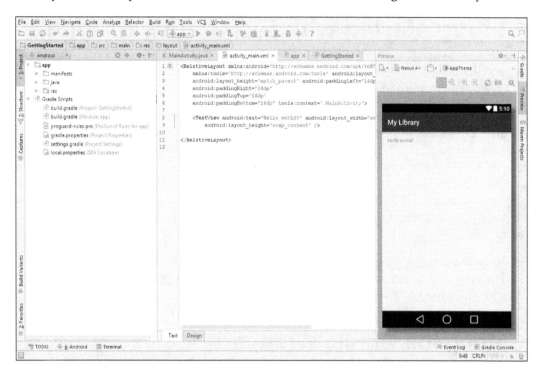

After you go through the entire wizard, Android Studio generates source code for an activity and a fragment, depending on the choices you made during the wizard. Android Studio also generates the basic Gradle files to make the project build. You will find a file called `settings.gradle` and one called `build.gradle` on the top level of the project. Inside the app module folder, there is another `build.gradle` file. We will go into more detail about the content and the purpose of these files in *Chapter 2, Basic Build Customization*.

You now have several options to trigger a build from inside Android Studio:

- Inside the **Build** menu, you can click on **Make Project**, or you can use the keyboard shortcut, which is *Ctrl + F9* on a PC and *Cmd + F9* on Mac OS X
- The toolbar has a shortcut for the same **Make Project**
- The Gradle tool window, which lists all the available Gradle tasks

In the Gradle tool window, you can try to execute `assembleDebug` to build, or `installDebug` to install the app on a device or emulator. We will discuss these tasks in the next part of this chapter, which deals with the Gradle wrapper.

Getting started with the Gradle Wrapper

Gradle is a tool that is under constant development, and new versions could potentially break backward compatibility. Using the Gradle Wrapper is a good way to avoid issues and to make sure builds are reproducible.

The Gradle Wrapper provides a batch file on Microsoft Windows and a shell script on other operating systems. When you run the script, the required version of Gradle is downloaded (if it is not present yet) and used automatically for the build. The idea behind this is that every developer or automated system that needs to build the app can just run the wrapper, which will then take care of the rest. This way, it is not required to manually install the correct version of Gradle on a developer machine or build server. Therefore, it is also recommended to add the wrapper files to your version control system.

Running the Gradle Wrapper is not that different from running Gradle directly. You just execute `gradlew` on Linux and Mac OS X and `gradlew.bat` on Microsoft Windows, instead of the regular `gradle` command.

Getting the Gradle Wrapper

For your convenience, every new Android project includes the Gradle Wrapper, so when you create a new project, you do not have to do anything at all to get the necessary files. It is, of course, possible to install Gradle manually on your computer and use it for your project, but the Gradle Wrapper can do the same things and guarantee that the correct version of Gradle is used. There is no good reason not to use the wrapper when working with Gradle outside of Android Studio.

You can check if the Gradle Wrapper is present in your project by navigating to the project folder and running `./gradlew -v` from the terminal or `gradlew.bat -v` from Command Prompt. Running this command displays the version of Gradle and some extra information about your setup. If you are converting an Eclipse project, the wrapper will not be present by default. In this case, it is possible to generate it using Gradle, but you will need to install Gradle first to get the wrapper.

The Gradle download page (http://gradle.org/downloads) has links to binaries and the source code, and it is possible to use a package manager such as Homebrew if you are on Mac OS X. All the instructions for installation are on the installation page (http://gradle.org/installation).

After you have downloaded and installed Gradle and added it to your PATH, create a build.gradle file containing these three lines:

```
task wrapper(type: Wrapper) {
    gradleVersion = '2.4'
}
```

After that, run gradle wrapper to generate the wrapper files.

In recent versions of Gradle, you can also run the wrapper task without modifying the build.gradle file, because it is included as a task by default. In that case, you can specify the version with the --gradle-version parameter, like this:

$ gradle wrapper --gradle-version 2.4

If you do not specify a version number, the wrapper is configured to use the Gradle version that the task is executed with.

These are all the files generated by the wrapper task:

```
myapp/
├── gradlew
├── gradlew.bat
└── gradle/wrapper/
    ├── gradle-wrapper.jar
    └── gradle-wrapper.properties
```

You can see here that the Gradle Wrapper has three parts:

- A batch file on Microsoft Windows and a shell script on Linux and Mac OS X
- A JAR file that is used by the batch file and shell script
- A properties file

The gradle-wrapper.properties file is the one that contains the configuration and determines what version of Gradle is used:

```
#Sat May 30 17:41:49 CEST 2015
distributionBase=GRADLE_USER_HOME
distributionPath=wrapper/dists
```

```
zipStoreBase=GRADLE_USER_HOME
zipStorePath=wrapper/dists
distributionUrl=https\://services.gradle.org/distributions/
gradle-2.4-all.zip
```

You can change the distribution URL if you want to use a customized Gradle distribution internally. This also means that any app or library that you use could have a different URL for Gradle, so be sure to check whether you can trust the properties before you run the wrapper.

Android Studio is kind enough to display a notification when the Gradle version used in a project is not up to date and will suggest automatically updating it for you. Basically, Android Studio changes the configuration in the `gradle-wrapper.properties` file and triggers a build, so that the latest version gets downloaded.

> Android Studio uses the information in the properties to determine which version of Gradle to use, and it runs the wrapper from the Gradle Wrapper directory inside your project. However, it does not make use of the shell or bash scripts, so you should not customize those.

Running basic build tasks

In the terminal or command prompt, navigate to the project directory and run the Gradle Wrapper with the `tasks` command:

```
$ gradlew tasks
```

This will print out a list of all the available tasks. If you add the `--all` parameter, you will get a more detailed overview with the dependencies for every task.

> On Microsoft Windows, you need to run `gradlew.bat`, and on Linux and Mac OS X, the full command is `./gradlew`. For the sake of brevity, we will just write `gradlew` throughout this book.

To build the project while you are developing, run the assemble task with the debug configuration:

```
$ gradlew assembleDebug
```

This task will create an APK with the debug version of the app. By default, the Android plugin for Gradle saves the APK in the directory `MyApp/app/build/outputs/apk`.

Abbreviated task names

To avoid a lot of typing in the terminal, Gradle also provides abbreviated Camel case task names as shortcuts. For example, you can execute `assembleDebug` by running `gradlew assDeb`, or even `gradlew aD`, from the command-line interface.

There is one caveat to this though. It will only work as long as the Camel case abbreviation is unique. As soon as another task has the same abbreviation, this trick does not work anymore for those tasks.

Besides `assemble`, there are three other basic tasks:

- `check` runs all the checks, this usually means running tests on a connected device or emulator
- `build` triggers both `assemble` and `check`
- `clean` cleans the output of the project

We will discuss these tasks in detail in *Chapter 2, Basic Build Customization*.

Migrating from Eclipse

There are two ways to take on migration from an Eclipse project to a Gradle-based project:

- Use the import wizard in Android Studio to handle migration automatically
- Add a Gradle script to the Eclipse project and set everything up manually

Most projects are simple enough for the import wizard to be able to convert everything automatically. If there is something the wizard cannot figure out, it might even give you hints as to what you need to change for it to work.

Some projects, though, might be extremely complicated and require a manual conversion. If you have a huge project and you prefer to convert the project in steps, instead of all at once, it is possible to execute Ant tasks, or even entire Ant builds from Gradle. Doing that, you can do the transition at the pace you prefer and convert all the components slowly.

Using the import wizard

To start the import wizard, you need to open Android Studio, click on the **File** menu and then on **Import Project...**, or on the Android Studio start screen, click on **Import Non-Android Studio project**.

If you convert a project with JAR files or library sources, the import wizard will suggest replacing those with Gradle dependencies. These dependencies can come from local Google repositories (such as the Android Support Library) or even from a known online repository central. If no matching Google or online dependencies are found, the JAR file is used, as it was before. The import wizard creates at least one module for your app. If you have libraries with source code in your project, those are converted to modules as well.

This is what the import wizard looks like:

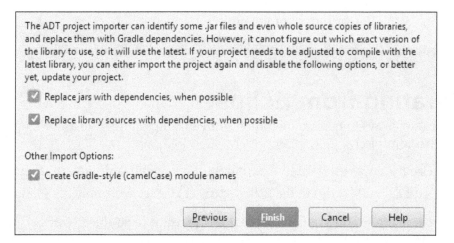

Studio creates a new folder to make sure you do not lose anything when you convert, and you can easily compare the outcome of the import wizard with the original. When the conversion is done, Android Studio opens the project and shows an import summary.

The summary lists any files that the import wizard decided to ignore and did not copy to the new project. If you want to include those anyway, you have to manually copy them to the new project. Right below the ignored files, the summary shows any JAR files that the import wizard was able to replace with Gradle dependencies. Android Studio tries to find those dependencies on JCenter. If you are using the Support Library, it is now included in the Google repository that is downloaded to your machine using the SDK manager, instead of a JAR file. Finally, the summary lists all the files that the import wizard has moved, showing their origin and destination.

The import wizard also adds three Gradle files: `settings.gradle` and `build.gradle` on the root, and another `build.gradle` in the module.

If you have any libraries that include source code, the import wizard turns those into Gradle projects as well and links everything together as necessary.

The project should now build without any issues, but keep in mind that you might need an Internet connection to download some of the necessary dependencies.

Projects that are more complicated might require extra work though, so next we will take a look at how to do the conversion manually.

The Eclipse export wizard

There is an export wizard in Eclipse as well, but it is completely outdated because the Android Tools team at Google stopped working on the Android Developer Tools for Eclipse. Therefore, it is recommended to always use the import wizard in Android Studio instead.

Migrating manually

There are multiple ways to go about manually migrating to a Gradle-based Android project. It is not required to change to the new directory structure, and it is even possible to run Ant scripts from your Gradle scripts. This makes the process of migrating very flexible, and it can make the transition easier for larger projects. We will look at running Ant tasks in *Chapter 9, Advanced Build Customization*.

Keeping the old project structure

If you do not want to move files around, it is possible to keep the Eclipse folder structure in your project. To do that, you need to change the source set configuration. We mentioned source sets earlier when talking about the project structure. Gradle and the Android plugin have their defaults, as usual, but it is possible to override those.

The first thing you need to do is to create a `build.gradle` file in the project directory. This file should apply the Android plugin and define the required properties for Gradle and the Android plugin. In its simplest form, it looks like this:

```
buildscript {
    repositories {
        jcenter()
    }
    dependencies {
```

```
        classpath 'com.android.tools.build:gradle:1.2.3'
    }
}

apply plugin: 'com.android.application'

android {
    compileSdkVersion 22
    buildToolsVersion "22.0.1"
}
```

Then you can start by changing the source set. Usually, overriding the main source set to comply with the Eclipse structure looks like this:

```
android {
  sourceSets {
    main {
      manifest.srcFile 'AndroidManifest.xml'
      java.srcDirs = ['src']
      resources.srcDirs = ['src']
      aidl.srcDirs = ['src']
      renderscript.srcDirs = ['src']
      res.srcDirs = ['res']
      assets.srcDirs = ['assets']
    }

  androidTest.setRoot('tests')
  }
}
```

In the Eclipse folder structure, all source files will reside in the same folder, so you need to tell Gradle that all these components can be found in the src folder. You only need to include the components that are in your project, but adding them all does no harm.

If you have any dependencies on JAR files, you need to tell Gradle where the dependencies are located. Assuming the JAR files are in a folder called libs, the configuration looks like this:

```
dependencies {
    compile fileTree(dir: 'libs', include: ['*.jar'])
}
```

This one-liner includes every file with the extension .jar inside the libs directory as a dependency.

Converting to the new project structure

If you decide to convert to the new project structure manually, you need to create a few folders and move some files. This table shows an overview of the most important files and folders, and where you need to move them to convert to the new project structure:

Old location	New location
`src/`	`app/src/main/java/`
`res/`	`app/src/main/res/`
`assets/`	`app/src/main/assets/`
`AndroidManifest.xml`	`app/src/main/AndroidManifest.xml`

If you have any unit tests, you need to move the source code for those to `app/src/test/java/` to have Gradle recognize them automatically. Functional tests belong in the `app/src/androidTest/java/` folder.

The next step is to create a `settings.gradle` file in the root of the project. This file needs to contain only one line, and its purpose is to tell Gradle to include the `app` module in the build:

```
include: ':app'
```

When that is ready, you need two `build.gradle` files for a successful Gradle build. The first one belongs in the root of the project (on the same level as `settings.gradle`) and is used to define project-wide settings:

```
buildscript {
    repositories {
        jcenter()
    }
    dependencies {
        classpath 'com.android.tools.build:gradle:1.2.3'
    }
}
```

This sets up a few properties for all modules in the project. The second `build.gradle` goes in the `app` folder and contains module-specific settings:

```
apply plugin: 'com.android.application'

android {
    compileSdkVersion 22
    buildToolsVersion "22.0.1"
}
```

These are the absolute basics. If you have a simple Android app that does not depend on third-party code, this will suffice. If you have any dependencies, you need to migrate those to Gradle as well.

Migrating libraries

If you have any libraries in your project that contain Android-specific code, those also need to use Gradle in order for them to play nice with the app module. The same basics apply, but you need to use the Android library plugin instead of the Android application plugin. The details of this process are discussed in *Chapter 5, Managing Multimodule Builds*.

Summary

We started the chapter by looking at the advantages of Gradle and why it is more useful than other build systems currently in use. We briefly looked at Android Studio and how it can help us by generating build files.

After the introduction, we took a look at the Gradle Wrapper, which makes maintenance and sharing projects a lot easier. We created a new project in Android Studio, and you now know how to migrate an Eclipse project to Android Studio and Gradle, both automatically and manually. You are also capable of building projects with Gradle in Android Studio, or straight from the command-line interface.

In the next few chapters, we will look at ways to customize the build, so you can further automate the build process and make maintenance even easier. We will start by examining all the standard Gradle files, exploring basic build tasks, and customizing parts of the build in the next chapter.

2
Basic Build Customization

We started out by looking at the uses of Gradle, and creating and converting Android projects. Now it is time to get a better understanding of the build files, to look at some useful tasks, and to explore the possibilities of both Gradle and the Android plugin.

In this chapter, we will look at the following topics:

- Understanding the Gradle files
- Getting started with build tasks
- Customizing the build

Understanding the Gradle files

When creating a new project with Android Studio, three Gradle files are generated by default. Two of those files, settings.gradle and build.gradle, end up on the top level of the project. Another build.gradle file is created in the Android app module. This is how the Gradle files are placed in the project:

```
MyApp
├── build.gradle
├── settings.gradle
└── app
    └── build.gradle
```

These three files each serve their own purpose, which we will further look into in the upcoming sections.

The settings file

For a new project containing only an Android app, `settings.gradle` looks like this:

```
include ':app'
```

The settings file is executed during the initialization phase, and defines which modules should be included in the build. In this example, the `app` module is included. Single module projects do not necessarily require a settings file, but multimodule projects do; otherwise, Gradle does not know which modules to include.

Behind the scenes, Gradle creates a `Settings` object for every settings file, and invokes the necessary methods from that object. You do not need to know the details of the `Settings` class, but it is good to be aware of this.

 A full explanation of the `Settings` class is out of the scope of this book. If you would like to know more, you can find a lot of information in the Gradle documentation (`https://gradle.org/docs/current/dsl/org.gradle.api.initialization.Settings.html`).

The top-level build file

The top-level `build.gradle` file is where you can configure options that need to be applied to all the modules in the project. It contains two blocks by default:

```
buildscript {
    repositories {
        jcenter()
    }
    dependencies {
        classpath 'com.android.tools.build:gradle:1.2.3'
    }
}

allprojects {
    repositories {
        jcenter()
    }
}
```

The `buildscript` block is where the actual build is configured. We looked at this briefly in *Chapter 1, Getting Started with Gradle and Android Studio*. The `repositories` block configures JCenter as a repository. In this case, a repository means a source of dependencies or, in other words, a list of downloadable libraries that we can use in our apps and libraries. JCenter is a well-known Maven repository.

The `dependencies` block is used to configure dependencies for the build process itself. This means that you should not include dependencies that you need for your applications or libraries in the top-level build file. The only dependency that is defined by default is the Android plugin for Gradle. This is required for every Android module, because it is this plugin that makes it possible to execute Android-related tasks.

The `allprojects` block can be used to define properties that need to be applied to all modules. You can take it even further and create tasks in the `allprojects` block. Those tasks will then be available in all modules.

As soon as you use `allprojects`, the modules are coupled to the project. This means that it will likely be impossible to build the modules separately, without the main project's build file. It might not seem like an issue at first, but later you might decide to separate an internal library into its own project, and then you will need to refactor your build files.

The module build file

The module-level `build.gradle` file contains options that only apply to the Android app module. It can also override any options from the top-level `build.gradle` file. The module build file looks like this:

```
apply plugin: 'com.android.application'

android {
    compileSdkVersion 22
    buildToolsVersion "22.0.1"

    defaultConfig {
        applicationId "com.gradleforandroid.gettingstarted"
        minSdkVersion 14
        targetSdkVersion 22
        versionCode 1
        versionName "1.0"
    }
```

```
    buildTypes {
        release {
            minifyEnabled false
            proguardFiles getDefaultProguardFile
              ('proguard-android.txt'), 'proguard-rules.pro'
        }
    }
}

dependencies {
    compile fileTree(dir: 'libs', include: ['*.jar'])
    compile 'com.android.support:appcompat-v7:22.2.0'
}
```

We will take a detailed look at the three main blocks.

Plugin

The first line applies the Android application plugin, which is configured as a dependency in the top-level build file, which we discussed earlier. The Android plugin is written and maintained by the Android Tools team at Google, and provides all tasks needed to build, test, and package Android applications and libraries.

Android

The biggest part of the build file is the `android` block. This block contains the entire Android-specific configuration, which is available through the Android plugin we applied earlier.

The only properties that are required are `compileSdkVersion` and `buildToolsVersion`:

- The first one, `compileSdkVersion`, is the API version of Android that you want to use to compile your app
- The second one, `buildToolsVersion`, is the version of build tools and compilers to use

The build tools contain command-line utilities, such as aapt, zipalign, dx, and renderscript; which are used to produce the various intermediate artifacts that make up your application. You can download the build tools through the SDK Manager.

The defaultConfig block configures core properties for the app. The properties in this block override the corresponding entries in the AndroidManifest.xml manifest file:

```
defaultConfig {
    applicationId "com.gradleforandroid.gettingstarted"
    minSdkVersion 14
    targetSdkVersion 22
    versionCode 1
    versionName "1.0"
}
```

The first property in this block is applicationId. This overrides the package name from the manifest file, but there are some differences between applicationId and the package name. Before Gradle was used as the default Android build system, the package name in AndroidManifest.xml had two purposes: it served as the unique identifier of an app, and it was used as the name for the package in the R resource class. Gradle makes it easier to create different versions of your app, using build variants. For example, it is very easy to make a free version and a paid version. These two versions need to have separate identifiers, so they appear as different apps on the Google Play Store, and can both be installed at the same time. The source code and generated R class, however, must retain the same package name at all times. Otherwise, all your source files would need to change, depending on the version you are building. That is why the Android Tools team has decoupled these two different usages of package name. The package, as defined in the manifest file, continues to be used in your source code and your R class, while the package name that is used by the device and Google Play as the unique identifier is now referred to as *application id*. This application ID will become a lot more interesting as we start experimenting with build types.

The next two properties in defaultConfig are minSdkVersion and targetSdkVersion. Both of these should look familiar because they have always been defined in the manifest as part of the <uses-sdk> element. The minSdkVersion setting is used to configure the minimum API level required to run the app. The targetSdkVersion setting informs the system that the app is tested on a specific version of Android, and that the operating system does not need to enable any forward-compatibility behavior. This has nothing to do with compileSdkVersion that we saw earlier.

The versionCode and versionName also have the same function as in the manifest file, and define a version number and a user-friendly version name for your app.

All values in the build file will override the values in the manifest file. It is therefore not required to define them in the manifest file if you define them in `build.gradle`. In case the build file does not contain a value, the manifest values will be used as a fallback.

The `buildTypes` block is where you define how to build and package the different build types of your app. We will take a detailed look at build types in *Chapter 4, Creating Build Variants*.

Dependencies

The `dependencies` block is a part of the standard Gradle configuration (that is why it is placed outside of the `android` block) and defines all dependencies for an app or library. By default, a new Android app has a dependency on all the JAR files in the `libs` directory. Depending on the options you select in the new project wizard, it might also depend on the `AppCompat` library. We will discuss dependencies in *Chapter 3, Managing Dependencies*.

Getting started with tasks

To know which tasks are available on a project, you can run `gradlew tasks`, which prints out a list of all the available tasks. In a newly created Android project, this includes Android tasks, build tasks, build setup tasks, help tasks, install tasks, verification tasks and other tasks. If you want to see not only the tasks, but also their dependencies, you can run `gradlew tasks --all`. It is possible to do a dry run of tasks, which prints out all the steps that are executed when running a specific task. This dry run will not actually perform any of these steps, so it is a safe way to see what you can expect to happen when running a certain task. You can do a dry run by adding the parameters `-m` or `--dry-run`.

Base tasks

The Android plugin for Gradle makes use of the Java base plugin, which in turn makes use of the base plugin. These add the standard lifecycle tasks and some common convention properties. The base plugin defines the tasks `assemble` and `clean`, and the Java base plugin defines the tasks `check` and `build`. These tasks are not implemented in the base plugin and do not perform any actions; they are used to define a convention for plugins that add the actual tasks that do the work.

The conventions for these tasks are:

- `assemble` assembles the output(s) of the project
- `clean` cleans the output of the project
- `check` runs all the checks, usually unit tests and instrumentation tests
- `build` runs both `assemble` and `check`

The Java base plugin also adds the concept of source sets. The Android plugin builds on these conventions, and thus exposes tasks that experienced Gradle users are used to seeing. On top of those base tasks, the Android plugin also adds a lot of Android-specific tasks.

Android tasks

The Android plugin extends the base tasks and implements their behavior. This is what the tasks do in an Android environment:

- `assemble` creates an APK for every build type
- `clean` removes all the build artifacts, such as the APK files
- `check` performs Lint checks and can abort the build if Lint detects an issue
- `build` runs both `assemble` and `check`

The `assemble` task depends on `assembleDebug` and `assembleRelease` by default, and more tasks if you add more build types. This means running `assemble` will trigger a build for every build type you have.

Besides extending these tasks, the Android plugin also adds a few new ones. These are the most significant new tasks:

- `connectedCheck` runs tests on a connected device or emulator
- `deviceCheck` is a placeholder task for other plugins to run tests on remote devices
- `installDebug` and `installRelease` install a specific version to a connected device or emulator
- All `install` tasks also have `uninstall` counterparts

The `build` task depends on `check`, but not on `connectedCheck` or `deviceCheck`. This is to make sure that regular checks do not require a connected device or running emulator. Running the check tasks generates a Lint report with a list of all warnings and errors, with a detailed explanation and a link to the related documentation. This report can be found in `app/build/outputs` and is called `lint-results.html`. It looks like this:

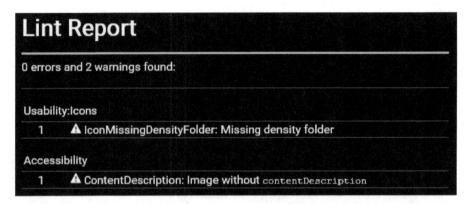

When you assemble a release, Lint will check for fatal issues that could cause the app to crash. If it finds any issues, it will abort the build and print the errors to the command-line interface. Lint will also generate a report in `app/build/outputs` in a file called `lint-results-release-fatal.html`. If you have multiple issues, going through the HTML report is more pleasant than scrolling back and forth in the command-line interface. The provided links are also extremely useful, because they take you to detailed explanations of the issues.

Inside Android Studio

You do not always have to run Gradle tasks from the command-line interface. Android Studio has a tool window that contains a list of all the available tasks. This tool window is called **Gradle** and looks like this:

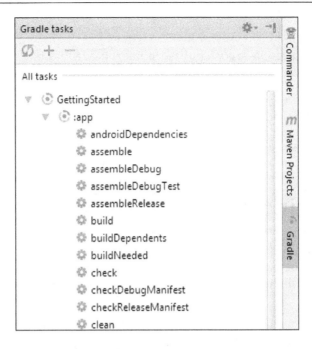

From this tool window, you can run a task simply by double-clicking on its name. You can follow the progress of any running task in the **Gradle Console** tool window. If you cannot find these tool windows, you can open them in the **View** menu, under **Tool Window**. This is what the Gradle Console tool window looks like:

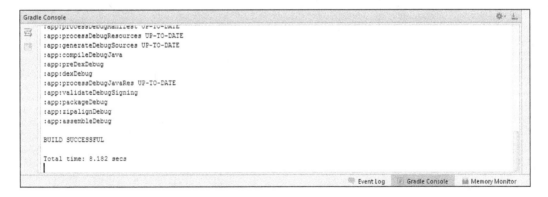

You can also run tasks from a command-line interface inside Android Studio, so you can do all app-related work inside the IDE if you like. To run the command, you need to open the **Terminal** tool window. This is a full-blown terminal, so it is possible to run any command from it. You might need to navigate to the top level of the project first, in order to work with the Gradle wrapper.

Changing the Android Studio terminal

It is possible to configure the terminal inside Android Studio to use a different shell. On Microsoft Windows, for example, the terminal defaults to Command Prompt. If you prefer to use the Git Bash (or any other shell) instead, open the Android Studio settings (under `File` and `Settings`) and look for **Terminal**. There you can change the shell path. For Git Bash on Microsoft Windows, it looks like this: `C:\Program Files (x86)\Git\bin\sh.exe --login -i.`

Customizing the build

There are a lot of ways to customize the build process, and when you are editing the build files in Android Studio, it is recommended to always sync the project with the Gradle files, no matter what you are customizing. This becomes especially important when you start adding dependencies or `BuildConfig` fields, which we will talk about soon.

Android Studio will show a message in the editor as soon as you edit `settings.gradle` or `build.gradle`, and it is possible to trigger the sync at all times by navigating to **Tools** | **Android** | **Sync Project with Gradle Files** or the corresponding button in the toolbar.

Under the hood, the Android Studio Sync actually runs the `generateDebugSources` task to generate all the necessary classes, based on the configuration in the build files.

Manipulating manifest entries

We already saw that it is possible to configure `applicationId`, `minSdkVersion`, `targetSdkVersion`, `versionCode`, and `versionName` directly from the build files, instead of in the manifest file. There are a few more properties that you can manipulate:

- `testApplicationId` is the application ID for the instrument test APK

- `testInstrumentationRunner` is the name of the JUnit test runner to be used for running your test (see *Chapter 6, Running Tests*)

- `signingConfig` (see *Chapter 4, Creating Build Variants*)

- `proguardFile` and `proguardFiles` (see *Chapter 9, Advanced Build Customization*)

Inside Android Studio

Instead of manually making changes in the build files, you can also change the basic settings in the **Project Structure** dialog in Android Studio. You can open the dialog from the **File** menu, and it enables you to edit project-wide settings and settings per module. For every Android module, you can change the standard Android plugin properties and all the manifest properties. In the following screenshot, you can see the properties for the release version of the app module in the **Project Structure** dialog:

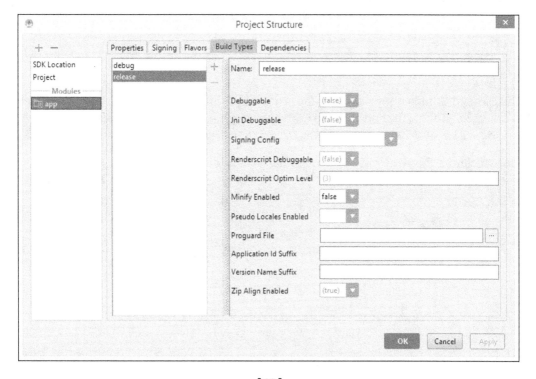

Be aware that if you make any changes in the **Project Structure** dialog, Android Studio will write the changes to the Gradle build configuration file.

BuildConfig and resources

Ever since SDK tools revision 17, the build tools generate a class called `BuildConfig`, which contains a `DEBUG` constant that is set according to the build type. This is useful if you have code that you only want to run when debugging, such as logging. It is possible through Gradle to extend that file so that you can have constants that contain different values in debug and release.

These constants are useful for toggling features or setting server URLs, for example:

```
android {
    buildTypes {
        debug {
            buildConfigField "String", "API_URL",
                "\"http://test.example.com/api\""
            buildConfigField "boolean", "LOG_HTTP_CALLS", "true"
        }

        release {
            buildConfigField "String", "API_URL",
                "\"http://example.com/api\""
            buildConfigField "boolean", "LOG_HTTP_CALLS", "false"
        }
    }
}
```

The escaped double quotes around the string value are necessary for it to be generated as an actual string. After adding the `buildConfigField` lines, it is possible to use `BuildConfig.API_URL` and `BuildConfig.LOG_HTTP` in your actual Java code.

More recently, the Android Tools team has also added the possibility to configure resources in a similar manner:

```
android {
    buildTypes {
        debug {
            resValue "string", "app_name", "Example DEBUG"
        }

        release {
            resValue "string", "app_name", "Example"
        }
    }
}
```

The escaped double quotes are not necessary here, because resource values are always wrapped with value="" by default.

Project-wide settings

If you have multiple Android modules in one project, it can be useful to apply settings to all of them without manually changing the build file for every module. We already saw how the allprojects block is used in the generated top-level build file to define repositories, and you can use the same strategy to apply Android-specific settings as well:

```
allprojects {
    apply plugin: 'com.android.application'

    android {
        compileSdkVersion 22
        buildToolsVersion "22.0.1"
    }
}
```

This will only work if all your modules are Android app projects though, because you need to apply the Android plugin to get access to the Android-specific settings. A better way to achieve this behavior is to define the values in the top-level build file, and then apply them in the modules. It is possible in Gradle to add extra ad hoc properties on the Project object. This means that any build.gradle file can define extra properties, and this happens in an ext block.

You can add an ext block with custom properties to the top-level build file:

```
ext {
    compileSdkVersion = 22
    buildToolsVersion = "22.0.1"
}
```

This makes it possible to use the properties in module-level build files using rootProject:

```
android {
    compileSdkVersion rootProject.ext.compileSdkVersion
    buildToolsVersion rootProject.ext.buildToolsVersion
}
```

Project properties

The `ext` block in the previous example is a way of defining extra properties. You can use properties to customize a build process on the fly, and we will make use of them when we start writing custom tasks in *Chapter 7, Creating Tasks and Plugins*. There are several ways to define properties, but we will only look at the three most used ones:

- The `ext` block
- The `gradle.properties` file
- The `-P` command-line parameter

Here is an example `build.gradle` file that incorporates those three ways of adding extra properties:

```
ext {
  local = 'Hello from build.gradle'
}

task printProperties << {
  println local          // Local extra property
  println propertiesFile          // Property from file
  if (project.hasProperty('cmd')) {
    println cmd          // Command line property
  }
}
```

This is the accompanying `gradle.properties` file (in the same folder):

```
propertiesFile = Hello from gradle.properties
```

> In the example, we create a new task. We will look at tasks and explain the syntax in *Chapter 7, Creating Tasks and Plugins*.

If you run the `printProperties` task with a command-line parameter, the output will look like this:

```
$ gradlew printProperties -Pcmd='Hello from the command line'
:printProperties
Hello from build.gradle
Hello from gradle.properties
Hello from the command line
```

Thanks to custom properties, changing the configuration of a build is as easy as changing a single property, or even just adding a command-line parameter.

 It is possible to define properties, both in the top-level build file and in the module build files. If a module defines a property that already exists in the top-level file, it will simply override it.

Default tasks

If you run Gradle without specifying a task, it runs the `help` task, which prints some information on how to work with Gradle. This happens because the help task is set as the default task. It is possible to override the default task and have a very common task, or even multiple tasks, run every time you execute Gradle without explicitly specifying the task.

To specify default tasks, add this line to the top-level `build.gradle` file:

```
defaultTasks 'clean', 'assembleDebug'
```

Now, when you run the Gradle wrapper without any parameters, it will run `clean` and `assembleDebug`. It is easy to see which tasks are set as default by running the `tasks` task and filtering the output.

```
$ gradlew tasks | grep "Default tasks"
Default tasks: clean, assembleDebug
```

Summary

In this chapter, we took a detailed look at the different Gradle files that are automatically generated by Android Studio. You are now able to create build files yourself, and add all the required fields and configure the key properties.

We got started with the basic build tasks, and learned how the Android plugin builds on the base plugin, and extends it with new Android-specific tasks. We also saw how to run build tasks both from the command-line interface, and from inside Android Studio.

In the final part of the chapter, we looked at several ways to influence the output of the build, and ways to configure parts of the build process itself.

In the last few years, the Android developer ecosystem has grown immensely, and a lot of interesting libraries have become available for everyone to use. In the next chapter, we will look at several ways to add dependencies to a project, so we can take advantage of this abundance of resources.

3
Managing Dependencies

Dependency management is one of the areas where Gradle really shines. In the best case scenario, all you need to do is add one line to your build file, and Gradle will download the dependency from a remote repository and make sure its classes are available to your project. Gradle even goes a step further. In case a dependency for your project has dependencies of its own, Gradle will resolve those, and take care of everything. These dependencies of dependencies are called **transitive dependencies**.

This chapter introduces the concepts of dependency management, and explains the multiple ways of adding dependencies to Android projects. These are the main topics we will be talking about:

- Repositories
- Local dependencies
- Dependency concepts

Repositories

When we discuss dependencies, we usually mean external dependencies, such as libraries that are provided by other developers. Manually managing dependencies can be a big hassle. You have to locate the library, download the JAR file, copy it into your project, and reference it. Often these JAR files have no version in their name, so you need to remember to add it yourself, in order to know when to update. You also need to make sure the libraries are stored in a source control system, so that the team members can work with the code base without manually downloading the dependencies themselves.

Using repositories can solve these issues. A repository can be seen as a collection of files. Gradle does not define any repositories for your project by default, so you need to add them to the `repositories` block. If you use Android Studio, this is done for you. We have mentioned the `repositories` block briefly in the previous chapters; it looks like this:

```
repositories {
    jcenter()
}
```

Gradle supports three different kinds of repositories: Maven, Ivy, and static files or directories. Dependencies are fetched from the repositories during the execution phase of the build. Gradle also keeps a local cache, so a particular version of a dependency only needs to be downloaded to your machine once.

A dependency is identified by three elements: group, name, and version. The group specifies the organization that created the library and is usually a reverse domain name. The name is a unique identifier for the library. The version specifies which version of the library you want to use. Using these three elements, a dependency can be declared in the `dependencies` block with the following structure:

```
dependencies {
    compile 'com.google.code.gson:gson:2.3'
    compile 'com.squareup.retrofit:retrofit:1.9.0'
}
```

This is shorthand for the full Groovy map notation, which looks like this:

```
dependencies {
    compile group: 'com.google.code.gson', name: 'gson', version:
    '2.3'
    compile group: 'com.squareup.retrofit', name: 'retrofit'
    version: '1.9.0'
}
```

 The only required field for a dependency is the name. Group and version are optional elements. Nonetheless, it is recommended to add the group for clarity, and the version in order to make sure libraries are not updated automatically, which could cause a build to break.

Preconfigured repositories

For your convenience, Gradle has preconfigured three Maven repositories: JCenter, Maven Central, and the local Maven repository. To include them in your build script, you need to include these lines:

```
repositories {
    mavenCentral()
    jcenter()
    mavenLocal()
}
```

Maven Central and JCenter are two well-known online repositories. There is no reason to use both of them at the same time, and it is always recommended to use JCenter, which is also the default repository in Android projects created with Android Studio. JCenter is a superset of Maven Central, so when you make the switch, you can leave your already defined dependencies intact. On top of that, it supports HTTPS, unlike Maven Central.

The local Maven repository is a local cache of all the dependencies you have used, and you can add your own dependencies as well. By default, the repository can be found in the home directory in a folder called .m2. On Linux or Mac OS X, the path is ~/.m2. On Microsoft Windows, it is %UserProfile%\.m2.

Besides these preconfigured repositories, you can also add other public, or even private repositories.

Remote repositories

Some organizations create interesting plugins or libraries, and prefer to host them on their own Maven or Ivy server, instead of publishing them to Maven Central or JCenter. To add those repositories to your build, all you need to do is to add the URL to a maven block.

```
repositories {
    maven {
        url "http://repo.acmecorp.com/maven2"
    }
}
```

The same goes for Ivy repositories. Apache Ivy is a dependency manager that is popular in the Ant world. Gradle supports these repositories in a format that is identical to the one that is used for Maven repositories. Add the repository URL to an `ivy` block, and you are good to go:

```
repositories {
    ivy {
        url "http://repo.acmecorp.com/repo"
    }
}
```

If your organization is running its own repository, chances are that it is secured, and you need credentials to access it. This is how you add credentials for a repository:

```
repositories {
    maven {
        url "http://repo.acmecorp.com/maven2"
        credentials {
            username 'user'
            password 'secretpassword'
        }
    }
}
```

The approach for Maven and Ivy is the same here as well. You can add a `credentials` block with the same format to the configuration of your Ivy repository.

Storing credentials

It is not a good idea to store your credentials in the build configuration file. The build configuration file is plain text, and is checked into the source control system. A better idea would be to use a separate Gradle properties file, as we have seen in *Chapter 2, Basic Build Customization.*

Local repositories

It is possible to run Maven and Ivy repositories on your own hard drive or a network drive. To add these to the build, you just need to configure the URL to a relative or absolute path to the location on the drive:

```
repositories {
    maven {
        url "../repo"
    }
}
```

New Android projects have a dependency on the Android Support Library by default. When installing the Google repositories using the SDK manager, two Maven repositories are created on your hard drive `ANDROID_SDK/extras/google/m2repository` and `ANDROID_SDK/extras/android/m2repository`. This is where Gradle gets the libraries provided by Google, such as the Android Support Library and Google Play Services.

You can add a regular directory as a repository as well, using `flatDirs`. This enables you to add files from that directory in the `dependency` block.

```
repositories {
    flatDir {
        dirs 'aars'
    }
}
```

Later in this chapter, when we talk about library projects, we will look at an example of how this can be used.

Local dependencies

In some cases, you might still need to manually download a JAR file or a native library. Perhaps you want to create your own library that you can reuse in several projects, without publishing it to a public or private repository. In those cases, it is impossible to use any of the online resources, and you will have to use different ways to add the dependencies. We will describe how to use file dependencies, how to include native libraries, and how you can include library projects in your project.

File dependencies

To add a JAR file as a dependency, you can use the `files` method that Gradle provides. This is what it looks like:

```
dependencies {
    compile files('libs/domoarigato.jar')
}
```

This can get tedious if you have a lot of JAR files, so it might be easier to add an entire folder at once:

```
dependencies {
    compile fileTree('libs')
}
```

By default, a newly created Android project will have a libs folder, and declare it to be used for dependencies. Instead of simply depending on all files in the folder, there is a filter that makes sure that only JAR files are used:

```
dependencies {
    compile fileTree(dir: 'libs', include: ['*.jar'])
}
```

This means that in any Android project that is created in Android Studio, you can drop a JAR in the libs folder, and it will automatically be included in the compile classpath and the final APK.

Native libraries

Libraries written in C or C++ can be compiled to platform-specific native code. These libraries typically consist of several .so files, one for every platform. The Android plugin supports native libraries by default, all you need to do is create a directory called jniLibs on the module level, and create subdirectories for each platform. Drop the .so files in the applicable directory, and you are good to go.

Your structure should look like this:

```
app
├── AndroidManifest.xml
└── jniLibs
    ├── armeabi
    │   └── nativelib.so
    ├── armeabi-v7a
    │   └── nativelib.so
    ├── mips
    │   └── nativelib.so
    └── x86
        └── nativelib.so
```

If this convention does not work for you, you can just set the location yourself in the build file:

```
android {
    sourceSets.main {
        jniLibs.srcDir 'src/main/libs'
    }
}
```

Library projects

If you want to share a library that uses Android APIs, or includes Android resources, you need to create a library project. Library projects generally behave the same as application projects. You can use the same tasks to build and test library projects, and they can have different build variants. The difference is in the output. Where an application project generates an APK that can be installed and run on an Android device, a library project generates a .aar file. This file can be used as a library for Android application projects.

Creating and using library project modules

Instead of applying the Android application plugin, the build script applies the Android library plugin:

```
apply plugin: 'com.android.library'
```

There are two ways to include a library project in your application. One is to have it as a module inside your project; another is to create a .aar file, which can be reused in multiple applications.

If you set up a library project as a module in your project, you need to add the module to settings.gradle and add it as a dependency to the application module. The settings file should look like this:

```
include ':app', ':library'
```

In this case, the library module is called library, and this corresponds to a folder with the same name. To use the library in the Android module, a dependency needs to be added to the build.gradle file of the Android module:

```
dependencies {
    compile project(':library')
}
```

This will include the output of the library in the classpath of the application module. We will look at this approach in more detail in *Chapter 5, Managing Multimodule Builds*.

Using .aar files

If you create a library that you want to reuse in different Android applications, you can build a .aar file, and add it to your project as a dependency. The .aar file will be generated in the build/output/aar/ folder of the module's directory when building the library. To add the .aar file as a dependency, you need to create a folder in the application module, copy the .aar file to it, and add the folder as a repository:

```
repositories {
    flatDir {
        dirs 'aars'
    }
}
```

This will make it possible to add any file inside that folder as a dependency. You can reference the dependency as follows:

```
dependencies {
    compile(name:'libraryname', ext:'aar')
}
```

This tells Gradle to look for a library with a certain name that has the .aar extension.

Dependency concepts

There are a few dependency-related concepts that are interesting to understand, even if you might not need to use them today. One of them is the concept of configurations, which explains the compile keyword that we have been using for dependencies throughout this chapter.

Configurations

Sometimes you might have to work with an SDK that is only present on certain devices, like a Bluetooth SDK from a specific vendor, for example. In order to be able to compile the code, you need to add the SDK to your compile classpath. You do not need to include the SDK in your APK though, because it is already on the device. This is where dependency configurations come in.

Gradle groups dependencies into configurations, which are just named sets of files. These are the standard configurations for an Android app or library:

- compile

- apk

- provided

- `testCompile`
- `androidTestCompile`

The `compile` configuration is the default one and contains all dependencies required to compile the main application. Everything in this configuration is not only added to the classpath, but also to the generated APK.

The dependencies in the `apk` configuration will only be added to the package, and are not added to the compilation classpath. The `provided` configuration does the exact opposite, and its dependencies will not be packaged. These two configurations only take JAR dependencies. Trying to add library projects to them will result in an error.

Finally, the `testCompile` and `androidTestCompile` configurations add extra libraries specifically for testing. These configurations are used when running test-related tasks, which can be useful when adding a testing framework such as JUnit or Espresso. You only want these frameworks to be present in the test APK, not in the release APK.

Besides those standard configurations, the Android plugin also generates configurations for every build variant, making it possible to add dependencies to configurations such as `debugCompile`, `releaseProvided`, and so on. This can be useful if you want to add a logging framework to only your debug builds, for example. You can find more information on this in *Chapter 4, Creating Build Variants*.

Semantic versioning

Versioning is an important aspect of dependency management. Dependencies added to repositories such as JCenter are assumed to follow a set of rules for versioning, called semantic versioning. With semantic versioning, a version number always has the format `major.minor.patch`, and the numbers are incremented according to the following rules:

- A major version goes up when you make incompatible API changes
- A minor version gets updated when you add functionality in a backwards-compatible manner
- A patch is incremented when you make bug fixes

Dynamic versions

In some situations, you might want to get the latest version of a dependency every time you build your app or library. The best way to accomplish this is by using dynamic versions. There are several ways to apply dynamic versions, here are some examples:

```
dependencies {
    compile 'com.android.support:support-v4:22.2.+'
    compile 'com.android.support:appcompat-v7:22.2+'
    compile 'com.android.support:recyclerview-v7:+'
}
```

In the first line, we tell Gradle to get the latest patch release. In line two, we specify that we want to get every new minor version, and it has to be at least minor version 2. In the last line, we tell Gradle always to get the newest version of the library.

You should be careful with using dynamic versions. If you allow Gradle to pick up the latest version, it might pick up a dependency version that is unstable, causing the build to break. Even worse, you could end up with different versions of a dependency on the build server and on your personal machine, causing your application's behavior to be inconsistent.

Android Studio will warn you about the possible problems with dynamic versions when you try to use it in your build file, as you can see in the following screenshot:

```
dependencies {
    compile fileTree(dir: 'libs', include: ['*.jar'])
    compile 'com.android.support:appcompat-v7:21.+'
}
```
Avoid using + in version numbers; can lead to unpredictable and unrepeatable builds (com.android.support:appcompat-v7:21.+) more... (Ctrl+F1)

Inside Android Studio

The easiest way to add new dependencies is to use Android Studio's **Project Structure** dialog. Open the dialog from the **File** menu and navigate to the **Dependencies** tab to get an overview of your current dependencies:

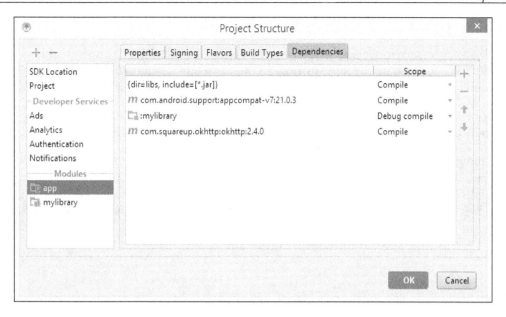

From this dialog, you can add new dependencies by clicking on the green plus icon. You can add other modules, files, and you can even search JCenter for libraries:

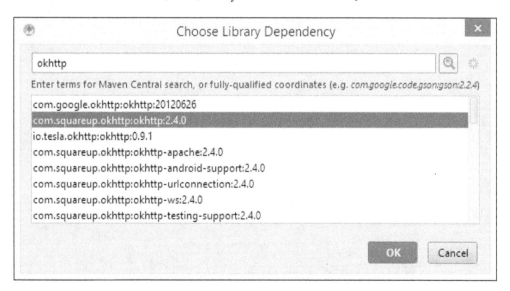

Using the Android Studio dialog makes it easy to get an overview of the dependencies in your project, and to add new libraries. You do not need to manually add lines to the `build.gradle` file, and it is easy to search JCenter straight from the IDE.

Summary

In this chapter, we looked at several ways to add dependencies to an Android project. We learned about repositories, all the forms they can come in, and how we can depend on files without using repositories.

You now also know about some important concepts regarding dependencies, namely configurations, semantic versioning, and dynamic versions.

We have mentioned build variants on several occasions already, and in the next chapter, we will finally explain what build variants are, and why they are useful. Build variants can make it easier to develop, test, and distribute apps. Understanding how variants work can significantly speed up your development and distribution process.

4
Creating Build Variants

When you are developing an app, you usually have a few different versions. The most common scenario is that you have a staging version that is used to manually test the app and assure its quality, and a production version. These versions usually have different settings. For example, the URL of the staging API can be different from the production API. In addition, you may have a free basic version of your app, and a paid version that has some extra features. In that case, you are already dealing with four different versions: staging free, staging paid, production free, and production paid. Having different configurations for every version can easily get very complicated.

Gradle has some convenient and extensible concepts to address this common issue. We already mentioned the `debug` and `release` build types that are created by Android Studio for every new project. There is another concept called product flavors, which adds even more possibilities for managing several versions of an app or library. Build types and product flavors are always combined, and make it easy to handle the scenario with free and paid versions of staging and production apps. The result of combining a build type and a product flavor is called a build variant.

We will start this chapter by looking at build types, what they can do to make a developer's life easier, and how to make the most of them. Then, we will discuss the difference between build types and product flavors and how both are used. We will also take a look at signing configurations, which is a necessity to publish apps, and how we can set a different signing configuration for every build variant.

In this chapter, we will cover the following topics:

- Build types
- Product flavors
- Build variants
- Signing configurations

Build types

In the Android plugin for Gradle, a build type is used to define how an app or library should be built. Every build type can specify whether the debug symbols should be included, what the application ID has to be, whether unused resources should be removed, and so on. You can define build types within a `buildTypes` block. This is what a standard `buildTypes` block looks like in a build file created by Android Studio:

```
android {
    buildTypes {
        release {
            minifyEnabled false
            proguardFiles getDefaultProguardFile
                ('proguard-android.txt'), 'proguard-rules.pro'
        }
    }
}
```

The default `build.gradle` file for a new module configures a build type called `release`. This build type does nothing more than disabling removal of unused resources (by setting `minifyEnabled` to `false`) and defining the location of the default ProGuard configuration file. This is to make it straightforward for developers to start using ProGuard for their production build, whenever they are ready for it.

The `release` build type is not the only build type that is already created for your project, though. By default, every module has a `debug` build type. It is set to sensible defaults, but you can change its configuration by including it in the `buildTypes` block, and overriding the properties you want to change.

> The `debug` build type has its own default settings to make it easy to debug. When you create your own build type, different defaults apply. For example, the `debuggable` property is set to `true` for the `debug` build type, but is set to `false` in any other build type you create.

Creating build types

When the default settings are not enough, it is easy to create your own custom build types. All that is required for a new build type is a new object within the `buildTypes` block. Here is an example of a custom build type called `staging`:

```
android {
    buildTypes {
```

```
        staging {
            applicationIdSuffix ".staging"
            versionNameSuffix "-staging"
            buildConfigField "String", "API_URL",
                "\"http://staging.example.com/api\""
        }
    }
}
```

The staging build type defines a new suffix for the application ID, making it different from the application ID of the debug and release versions. Assuming you have the default build configuration, plus the staging build type, the application IDs for the build types look like this:

- Debug: com.package
- Release: com.package
- Staging: com.package.staging

This means that you will be able to install both the staging version and the release version on the same device without causing any conflicts. The staging build type also has a version name suffix, which is useful to differentiate several versions of the app on the same device. The buildConfigField property defines a custom URL for the API, using a build configuration field, as we saw in *Chapter 2, Basic Build Customization*.

You do not always have to start from scratch when creating a new build type. It is possible to initialize a build type that copies the properties of another build type:

```
android {
    buildTypes {
        staging.initWith(buildTypes.debug)
        staging {
            applicationIdSuffix ".staging"
            versionNameSuffix "-staging"
            debuggable = false
        }
    }
}
```

The initWith() method creates a new build type and copies all properties from an existing build type to the newly created one. It is possible to override properties or define extra properties by simply defining them in the new build type object.

Source sets

When you create a new build type, Gradle also creates a new source set. By default, the source set directory is assumed to have the same name as the build type. The directory is not automatically created when you define a new build type, though. You have to create the source set directory yourself before you can use custom source code and resources for a build type.

This is what the directory structure can look like with the standard `debug` and `release` build type, plus an extra staging build type:

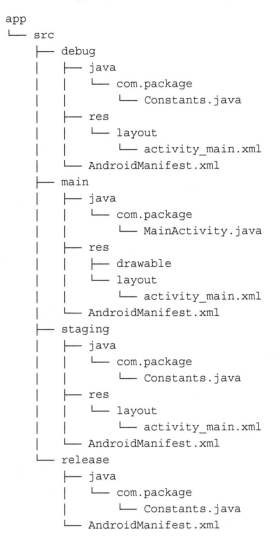

```
app
└── src
    ├── debug
    │   ├── java
    │   │   └── com.package
    │   │       └── Constants.java
    │   ├── res
    │   │   └── layout
    │   │       └── activity_main.xml
    │   └── AndroidManifest.xml
    ├── main
    │   ├── java
    │   │   └── com.package
    │   │       └── MainActivity.java
    │   ├── res
    │   │   ├── drawable
    │   │   └── layout
    │   │       └── activity_main.xml
    │   └── AndroidManifest.xml
    ├── staging
    │   ├── java
    │   │   └── com.package
    │   │       └── Constants.java
    │   ├── res
    │   │   └── layout
    │   │       └── activity_main.xml
    │   └── AndroidManifest.xml
    └── release
        ├── java
        │   └── com.package
        │       └── Constants.java
        └── AndroidManifest.xml
```

These source sets open up a world of possibilities. For example, you can override certain properties for specific build types, add custom code to certain build types, and add customized layouts or strings to different build types.

 When adding Java classes to build types, it is important to keep in mind that this process is mutually exclusive. This means that if you add class CustomLogic.java to the staging source set, you will be able to add the same class to the debug and release source sets, but not to the main source set. The class would then be defined twice, throwing an exception when you try to build.

Resources are handled in a special way when using different source sets. Drawables and layout files will completely override the resources with the same name in the main source set, but files in the values directory (such as strings.xml) will not. Gradle will instead merge the content of the build type resources with the main resources.

For example, if you have a strings.xml file in the main source set that looks like this:

```
<resources>
    <string name="app_name">TypesAndFlavors</string>
    <string name="hello_world">Hello world!</string>
</resources>
```

And if you have a strings.xml file in the staging build type source set like this:

```
<resources>
    <string name="app_name">TypesAndFlavors STAGING</string>
</resources>
```

Then, the merged strings.xml file will look like this:

```
<resources>
    <string name="app_name">TypesAndFlavors STAGING</string>
    <string name="hello_world">Hello world!</string>
</resources>
```

When you build a build type that is not staging, the final strings.xml file will just be the strings.xml file from the main source set.

The same is true for manifest files. If you create a manifest file for a build type, you do not need to copy the entire manifest file from the main source set; you can just add the tags you need. The Android plugin will merge the manifests together.

We will talk about merging in more detail later in this chapter.

Dependencies

Every build type can have its own dependencies. Gradle automatically creates new dependency configurations for every build type. If you want to add a logging framework only for debug builds, for example, you can do it like this:

```
dependencies {
    compile fileTree(dir: 'libs', include: ['*.jar'])
    compile 'com.android.support:appcompat-v7:22.2.0'
    debugCompile 'de.mindpipe.android:android-logging-log4j:1.0.3'
}
```

You can combine any build type with any dependency configuration in this manner. This gives you the possibility to get very specific with dependencies.

Product flavors

As opposed to build types, which are used to configure several different builds of the same app or library, product flavors are used to create different versions of the same app. The typical example is an app that has a free and a paid version. Another common scenario is an agency that builds apps that have the same functionality for several clients, where only the branding changes. This is very common in the taxi industry or with banking apps, where one company creates an app that can be reused for all clients in the same category. The only things that change are the main colors, the logo, and the URL of the backend. Product flavors greatly simplify the process of having different versions of an app based on the same code.

If you are unsure whether you need a new build type, or a new product flavor, you should ask yourself if you want to create a new build of the same app for internal use, or a new APK to publish to Google Play. If you need an entirely new app that needs to be published separately from what you already have, then product flavors are the way to go. Otherwise, you should stick to using build types.

Creating product flavors

Creating product flavors is very similar to creating build types. You can create a new product flavor by adding it to the productFlavor block, like this:

```
android {
    productFlavors {
        red {
            applicationId 'com.gradleforandroid.red'
            versionCode 3
        }
```

```
    blue {
        applicationId 'com.gradleforandroid.blue'
        minSdkVersion 14
        versionCode 4
    }
  }
}
```

Product flavors have different properties than build types. That is because product flavors are objects of the `ProductFlavor` class, just like the `defaultConfig` object that is present in all build scripts. This means that `defaultConfig` and all your product flavors share the same properties.

Source sets

Just like with build types, product flavors can have their own source set directories. Creating a folder for a specific flavor is as easy as creating a folder with the flavor name. You can even go one step further and create a folder specifically for a combination of a certain build type and flavor. The name of the folder would then be the flavor name followed by the build type name. For example, if you want to have a different app icon specifically for the release version of the blue flavor, the folder would have to be called `blueRelease`. The components of the combined folder will have a higher priority than the components from both the build type folder and the product flavor folder.

Multiflavor variants

In some cases, you might want to take it further and create combinations of product flavors. For example, client A and client B might each want free and paid versions of their app, which is based on the same code base, but has different branding. Creating four different flavors would mean having several duplicate settings, so that is not the way to go. Combining flavors in an efficient way is possible using flavor dimensions, like this:

```
android {
    flavorDimensions "color", "price"

    productFlavors {
        red {
            flavorDimension "color"
        }
```

```
        blue {
            flavorDimension "color"
        }
        free {
            flavorDimension "price"
        }

        paid {
            flavorDimension "price"
        }
    }
}
```

As soon as you add the flavor dimensions, Gradle expects you to specify a dimension for each flavor. If you forget, you will get a build error with a message explaining the issue. The `flavorDimensions` array defines the dimensions, and the order of the dimensions is very important. When combining two flavors, they might have defined the same properties or resources. In that case, the order of the flavor dimensions array determines which flavor configuration overrides the other. In the earlier example, the color dimension overrides the price dimension. The order also determines the name of the build variant.

Assuming the default build configuration with the debug and release build types, defining the flavors as shown in the previous example will generate all of these build variants:

- `blueFreeDebug` and `blueFreeRelease`
- `bluePaidDebug` and `bluePaidRelease`
- `redFreeDebug` and `redFreeRelease`
- `redPaidDebug` and `redPaidRelease`

Build variants

Build variants are simply the result of combining build types and product flavors. Whenever you create a build type or product flavor, new variants are created as well. For example, if you have the standard `debug` and `release` build types, and you create a red and blue product flavor, the following build variants will be generated:

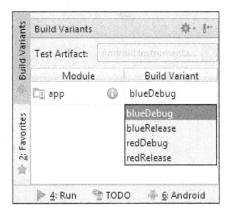

This is a screenshot of the **Build Variants** tool window in Android Studio. You can find the tool window in the bottom-left corner of the editor, or open it from **View** | **Tool Windows** | **Build Variants**. This tool window lists all the build variants, but also allows you to switch between them. Changing the selected build variant here will affect which variant runs when the **Run** button is clicked.

If you have no product flavors, variants will simply consist of build types. It is impossible to not have any build types. Even if you do not define any build types yourself, the Android plugin for Gradle always creates a debug build type for your app or library.

Tasks

The Android plugin for Gradle will create tasks for every build variant you configure. A new Android app has debug and release build types by default, so you already have assembleDebug and assembleRelease to build both APKs separately, and assemble to create both with a single command. When you add a new build type, a new task will be created as well. As soon as you start adding flavors into the mix, a whole new range of tasks is created, because the tasks for every build type are combined with tasks for every product flavor. This means that for a simple setup with one build type and one flavor, you already have three tasks to build all the variants:

- assembleBlue uses the blue flavor configuration and assembles both BlueRelease and BlueDebug.

- assembleDebug uses the debug build type configuration and assembles a debug version for every product flavor.

- `assembleBlueDebug` combines the flavor configuration with the build type configuration, and the flavor settings override the build type settings.

New tasks are created for every build type, for every product flavor, and for every combination of build type and product flavor.

Source sets

Build variants that are a combination of a build type and one or more product flavors can also have their own source set directories. For example, the variant created from the `debug` build type, the blue flavor and the free flavor, can have its own source set in `src/blueFreeDebug/java/`. It is possible to override the location for the directory using the `sourceSets` block, which we saw in *Chapter 1, Getting Started with Gradle and Android Studio.*

Resource and manifest merging

The introduction of source sets adds extra complexity to the build process. The Android plugin for Gradle needs to merge the main source set and the build type source sets together before packaging the app. In addition, library projects can also provide extra resources, and those need to be merged in as well. The same goes for manifest files. You may need extra Android permissions in the debug variant of your app to store log files, for example. You do not want to declare this permission on the main source set because that might scare potential users. Instead, you would add an extra manifest file in the `debug` build type source set to declare the extra permission.

The priority order for resources and manifests looks like this:

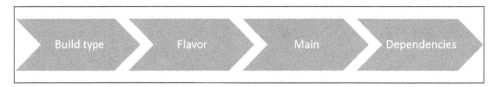

If a resource is declared in a flavor and in the main source set, the one from the flavor will be given a higher priority. In this case, the resource in the flavor source set will be packaged, and not the one in the main source set. Resources declared in library projects always have the lowest priority.

There is a lot more to learn about resource and manifest merging. It is an incredibly complicated subject, and if we were to explain its details, we would need to dedicate an entire chapter to it. Instead, if you want to learn more, it is a good idea to read the official documentation on the topic at `http://tools.android.com/tech-docs/new-build-system/user-guide/manifest-merger`.

Creating build variants

Gradle makes it easy to handle the complexity of build variants. Even when creating and configuring two build types and two product flavors, the build file is still concise:

```
android {
    buildTypes {
        debug {
            buildConfigField "String", "API_URL",
                "\"http://test.example.com/api\""
        }

        staging.initWith(android.buildTypes.debug)
        staging {
            buildConfigField "String", "API_URL",
                "\"http://staging.example.com/api\""
            applicationIdSuffix ".staging"
        }
    }

    productFlavors {
        red {
            applicationId "com.gradleforandroid.red"
            resValue "color", "flavor_color", "#ff0000"
        }

        blue {
            applicationId "com.gradleforandroid.blue"
            resValue "color", "flavor_color", "#0000ff"
        }
    }
}
```

In this example, we have created four different build variants: `blueDebug`, `blueStaging`, `redDebug`, and `redStaging`. Each variant has its own combination of API URL and flavor color. This is what `blueDebug` looks like on a phone:

And this is the `redStaging` variant of the same app:

The first screenshot shows the `blueDebug` variant, which uses the URL defined in the `debug` build type, and makes its text blue, based on `flavor_color` defined for the blue product flavor. The second screenshot shows `redStaging`, with the staging URL and red text. The red staging version also has a different app icon, because the drawable folders in the source set for the `staging` build type have their own app icon images.

Variant filters

It is possible to entirely ignore certain variants in your build. This way, you can speed up the process of building all variants with the general `assemble` command, and your list of tasks will not be polluted with tasks that should not be executed. This also ensures that the build variant does not show up in the Android Studio build variants switcher.

You can filter out variants, using this code in the root level of the `build.gradle` file of your app or library:

```
android.variantFilter { variant ->
    if(variant.buildType.name.equals('release')) {
        variant.getFlavors().each() { flavor ->
            if (flavor.name.equals('blue')) {
```

```
                    variant.setIgnore(true);
            }
        }
    }
}
```

In this example, we first check if the variant's build type has the name `release`. Then, we extract the names of all the product flavors. When using flavors without dimensions, there is only one product flavor in the flavors array. As soon as you start applying flavor dimensions, the flavor array will hold as many flavors as there are dimensions. In the example script, we check for the blue product flavor, and tell the build script to ignore this particular variant.

This is the result of the variant filter in the build variant switcher in Android Studio:

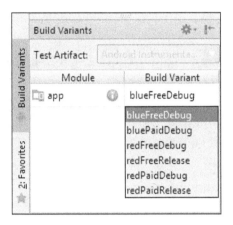

You can see that the two blue release variants (`blueFreeRelease` and `bluePaidRelease`) are filtered out of the list of build variants. If you were to run `gradlew tasks` now, you would notice that all the tasks related to those variants do not exist anymore.

Signing configurations

Before you can publish an app on Google Play or any other app store, you need to sign it with a private key. If you have a paid and free version or different apps for different clients, you need to sign every flavor with a different key. This is where signing configurations come in handy.

Signing configurations can be defined like this:

```
android {
    signingConfigs {
        staging.initWith(signingConfigs.debug)

        release {
            storeFile file("release.keystore")
            storePassword"secretpassword"
            keyAlias "gradleforandroid"
            keyPassword "secretpassword"
        }
    }
}
```

In this example, we create two different signing configurations.

The debug configuration is automatically set up by the Android plugin and makes use of a general keystore with a known password, so it is not necessary to create a signing configuration for this build type.

The staging configuration in the example uses `initWith()`, which copies all properties from another signing configuration. This means that the staging builds are signed with the debug key, instead of defining its own.

The release configuration uses `storeFile` to specify the path of the keystore file and then defines the key alias and both passwords.

 As mentioned earlier, it is not a good idea to store credentials in the build configuration file. A better idea would be to use a Gradle properties file. In *Chapter 7, Creating Tasks and Plugins*, there is an entire section dedicated to a task to deal with signing configuration passwords.

After you define the signing configurations, you need to apply them to your build types or flavors. Build types and flavors both have a property called `signingConfig`, which can be used like this:

```
android {
    buildTypes {
        release {
            signingConfig signingConfigs.release
        }
    }
}
```

This example uses build types, but if you want to use different certificates for every flavor you create, you need to create different signing configurations. You can define those in the exact same way:

```
android {
    productFlavors {
        blue {
            signingConfig signingConfigs.release
        }
    }
}
```

Using signing configurations this way leads to problems though. When assigning a configuration to a flavor, you are actually overriding the signing configurations for the build types. What you want to do instead, when using flavors, is to have a different key per build type per flavor:

```
android {
    buildTypes {
        release {
            productFlavors.red.signingConfig signingConfigs.red
            productFlavors.blue.signingConfig signingConfigs.blue
        }
    }
}
```

The example shows how to use different signing configurations for the red and blue flavors that use the release build type, without influencing the debug and staging build types.

Summary

In this chapter, we talked about build types, product flavors, and all their possible combinations. These are very powerful tools that can be used in any application. From a simple setup with different URLs and keys to more complicated apps that share the same source code and resources but have different branding and several versions; build types and product flavors can make your life considerably easier.

We also talked about signing configurations and applying them, and mentioned a common pitfall when signing product flavors.

Next, you will be introduced to multimodule builds. These are useful when you want to extract code into a library or a library project, or when you want to include, for example, an Android Wear module into your app.

5
Managing Multimodule Builds

Android Studio allows you to create modules for not just apps and libraries, but also for Android Wear, Android TV, Google App Engine, and more. All of these modules can be used together in a single project. For example, you might want to create an app that uses Google Cloud Endpoints for the backend and includes integration with Android Wear. In that case, you could have a project with three different modules: one for the app, one for the backend, and one for the Android Wear integration. Knowing how multimodule projects are structured and built can speed up your development cycle significantly.

The documentation for Gradle and the Gradle Android plugin both use the term multiproject builds. In Android Studio, however, there is a distinction between a *module* and a *project*. A module can be an Android app or a Google App Engine backend, for example. A project, on the other hand, is a collection of modules. In this book, we use the terms module and project in the same way the IDE does, to avoid confusion. Keep this in mind when you browse through the documentation.

In this chapter, we will cover the theory of multimodule builds, and then show some examples that can be useful in real-life projects:

- Anatomy of a multimodule build
- Adding modules to a project
- Tips and best practices

The anatomy of a multimodule build

Usually, a multimodule project works by having a root directory that contains all modules in subdirectories. To tell Gradle how the project is structured, and which directories contain modules, you need to provide a `settings.gradle` file in the root of the project. Each module can then provide its own `build.gradle` file. We already learned how `settings.gradle` and the `build.gradle` files work in *Chapter 2, Basic Build Customization*, so here we will just focus on how to use them for multimodule projects.

This is what a multimodule project could look like:

```
project
├── setting.gradle
├── build.gradle
├── app
│   └── build.gradle
└── library
    └── build.gradle
```

This is the simplest and most straightforward way to set up a project with multiple modules. The `settings.gradle` file declares all the modules in the project and looks like this:

```
include ':app', ':library'
```

This makes sure that the app and library modules are included in the build configuration. All you need to do is to add the name of the directory of the module.

To add the library module as a dependency to the app module, you need to add this to the `build.gradle` file of the app module:

```
dependencies {
    compile project(':library')
}
```

In order to add a dependency on a module, you need to use the `project()` method, with the module path as the parameter.

If you want to use subdirectories to organize your modules, Gradle can be configured to suit your needs. For example, you could have a directory structure that looks like this:

```
project
├── setting.gradle
├── build.gradle
```

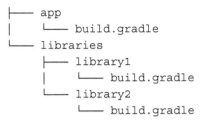

```
├── app
│    └── build.gradle
└── libraries
      ├── library1
      │    └── build.gradle
      └── library2
            └── build.gradle
```

The app module is still located in the root as it was earlier, but the project now has two different libraries. These library modules are not located in the project root directory, but in a specific libraries directory. With this directory structure, you can declare the app and library modules in `settings.gradle` like this:

```
include ':app', ':libraries:library1', ':libraries:library2'
```

Notice how easy it is to declare modules within a subdirectory. All paths are relative to the root directory (where the `settings.gradle` file is). The colon is used as a replacement for the forward slash in the path.

When adding a module in a subdirectory as a dependency to another module, you should always reference it from the root. This means that if the app module in the previous example depends on `library1`, the `build.gradle` file for the app module should look like this:

```
dependencies {
    compile project(':libraries:library1')
}
```

If you declare dependencies in a subdirectory, all paths should still be relative to the root directory. The reason for this is that Gradle constructs your project's dependency model starting at the root of the project.

The build lifecycle revisited

Knowing how the build process model is constructed makes it easier to understand how multimodule projects are composed. We already talked about the build lifecycle in *Chapter 1, Getting Starting with Gradle and Android Studio*, so you already know the basics, but some details are important specifically for multimodule builds.

In the first phase, the initialization phase, Gradle looks for a `settings.gradle` file. If this file does not exist, Gradle assumes that you have a single module build. If you have multiple modules though, the settings file is where you can define the subdirectories that contain the individual modules. If those subdirectories contain their own `build.gradle` files, Gradle will process those, and merge them into the build process model. This explains why you should always declare dependencies on a module with a path relative to the root directory. Gradle will always try to figure out dependencies from the root.

Once you understand how the build process model is put together, it becomes clear that there are several strategies to configure multimodule project builds. You could configure the settings for all the modules in a `build.gradle` file in the root directory. This makes it easy to get an overview of the entire build configuration for a project, but it could get very messy, especially when you have modules that require different plugins that each have their own DSL. Another way is to have `build.gradle` files separately for every module. This strategy makes sure that the modules are not tightly coupled to each other. It also makes it easier to track build changes, because you do not need to figure out which change applies to which module.

The last strategy is the hybrid approach. You can have a build file in the root of the project to define common properties for all modules, and a build file per module to configure settings that apply only to that specific module. Android Studio follows this approach. It creates a `build.gradle` file in the root directory, and another `build.gradle` file for the module.

Module tasks

As soon as you have multiple modules in your project, you need to think twice before running tasks. When you run a task from the root of the project in the command-line interface, Gradle will figure out which modules have a task with that name and execute it for every module. For example, if you have one mobile app module and one Android Wear module, running `gradlew assembleDebug` will build the debug version of both the mobile app module and the Android Wear module. When you change the directory to one of the modules, however, Gradle will only run the tasks for that particular module, even when you use the Gradle wrapper in the root of the project. For example, running `../gradlew assembleDebug` from the Android Wear module directory will only build the Android Wear module.

Switching directories to run module-specific tasks can get annoying. Luckily, there is another way. You can prepend a task name with the module name to run the task only on that specific module. For example, to build the Android Wear module only, you can use the `gradlew :wear:assembleDebug` command.

Adding modules to a project

Adding a new module is as simple as going through a wizard in Android Studio. The wizard also sets up the basics of the build file. In some cases, adding a module will even cause Android Studio to edit the build file of your app module. For example, when adding an Android Wear module, the IDE assumes that you want to use it for your Android app, and add a line in the build file to reference the Android Wear module.

This is what the **New Module** dialog in Android Studio looks like:

In the following sections, we will show different modules that can be added to an Android project with Android Studio, explain their custom properties, and specify how they alter the build process.

Adding a Java library

When you add a new Java library module, the `build.gradle` file generated by Android Studio looks like this:

```
apply plugin: 'java'

dependencies {
    compile fileTree(dir: 'libs', include: ['*.jar'])
}
```

Java library modules use the Java plugin instead of the Android plugins we are used to seeing. This means that a lot of Android-specific properties and tasks are not available, but you do not need those for a Java library anyway.

The build file also has basic dependency management set up, so you can add JAR files to your `libs` folder without needing any special configuration. You can add more dependencies, using what you learned in *Chapter 3, Managing Dependencies*. The dependency configuration does not depend on the Android plugin.

To add a Java library module named `javalib` as a dependency to your app module, for example, simply add this line to the build configuration file for the app module:

```
dependencies {
    compile project(':javalib')
}
```

This tells Gradle to import a module named `javalib` in the build. If you add this dependency in your app module, the `javalib` module will always be built before the build for the app module itself is started.

Adding an Android library

We briefly mentioned Android libraries in *Chapter 3, Managing Dependencies*, where we called them library projects. Both names are used throughout the documentation and in various tutorials. In this section, we will use the name `Androidlibrary` because that is the name used in the **New Module** dialog in Android Studio.

The default `build.gradle` file for an Android library starts with this line:

```
apply plugin: 'com.android.library'
```

Adding a dependency on an Android library module is done in the exact same way as with Java libraries:

```
dependencies {
    compile project(':androidlib')
}
```

An Android library contains not only the Java code of the library, but also all Android resources, such as the manifest, strings, and layouts. After referencing an Android library in your app, you can use all of the library's classes and resources in the app.

Integrating Android Wear

If you are looking to add deep integration of your app to Android Wear, you will need to add an Android Wear module. It is interesting to note that Android Wear modules also use the Android application plugin. This means that all build properties and tasks are available.

The only part of the build.gradle file that is different from a regular Android app module is the dependency configuration:

```
dependencies {
    compile fileTree(dir: 'libs', include: ['*.jar'])
    compile 'com.google.android.support:wearable:1.1.0'
    compile 'com.google.android.gms:play-services-wearable:6.5.87'
}
```

Every Android Wear app depends on a few Android Wear-specific libraries provided by Google. In order to use an Android Wear app with your Android app, you need to package it with the app. You can do this by adding a dependency in the Android app:

```
dependencies {
    wearApp project(':wear')
}
```

The wearApp configuration makes sure that the APK of the Wear module is added to the final APK of the Android app and does the necessary configuration for you.

Using Google App Engine

Google App Engine is a cloud computing platform that you can use to host web applications, without having to set up your own server. It is free to use up to a certain usage level, which makes it a good environment for experimentation. Google App Engine also provides a service called Cloud Endpoints, which is used to create RESTful services. Using Google App Engine with Cloud Endpoints makes it easy to build a backend for your apps. The App Engine Gradle plugin makes it even easier by generating a client library for your Android app, meaning you do not need to write any of the API-related code yourself. This makes Google App Engine an interesting option for an app backend, so in the following section we will look at how the App Engine Gradle plugin works, and how we can make use of Cloud Endpoints.

To create a new Google App Engine module with Cloud Endpoints, open the **New Module** dialog from **File | New Module...** and select **Google Cloud Module**. When setting up the module, you can change the type to include Cloud Endpoints. Then, select the client module that will be using this backend.

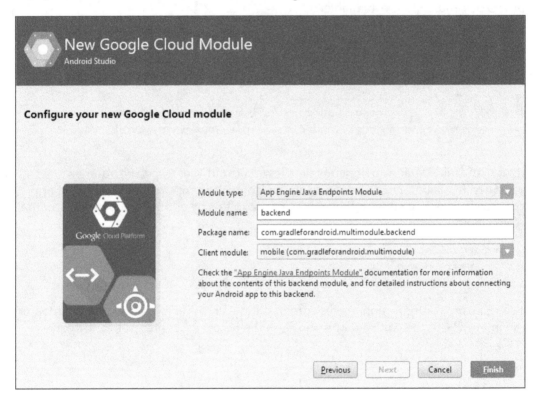

A thorough explanation of Google App Engine and Cloud Endpoints is beyond the scope of this book; we will only look at the Gradle integration in both the App Engine module and the client app module.

Analyzing the build file

The `build.gradle` file for this module becomes quite big, so we will only look at the most interesting parts, beginning with the new build script dependency:

```
buildscript {
    dependencies {
        classpath 'com.google.appengine:gradle-appengine-
            plugin:1.9.18'
    }
}
```

The App Engine plugin needs to be defined in `classpath` of the build script. We have seen this earlier when adding the Android plugin. When that is in place, we can apply the App Engine plugin along with two other plugins:

```
apply plugin: 'java'
apply plugin: 'war'
apply plugin: 'appengine'
```

The Java plugin is primarily used to generate JAR files for Cloud Endpoints. The WAR plugin is necessary to run and distribute the entire backend. The WAR plugin generates a WAR file, which is how Java web applications are distributed. Finally, the App Engine plugin adds a number of tasks to build, run, and deploy the entire backend.

The next important block defines the dependencies of the App Engine module:

```
dependencies {
    appengineSdk 'com.google.appengine:appengine-java-sdk:1.9.18'
    compile 'com.google.appengine:appengine-endpoints:1.9.18'
    compile 'com.google.appengine:appengine-endpoints-deps:1.9.18'
    compile 'javax.servlet:servlet-api:2.5'
}
```

The first dependency uses `appengineSdk` to specify which SDK should be used in this module. The `endpoints` dependencies are necessary for Cloud Endpoints to work. These are only added if you choose to use Cloud Endpoints in your module. The servlet dependency is a requirement for any Google App Engine module.

Configure any App Engine–specific settings in the `appengine` block:

```
appengine {
    downloadSdk = true
    appcfg {
        oauth2 = true
    }
    endpoints {
        getClientLibsOnBuild = true
        getDiscoveryDocsOnBuild = true
    }
}
```

Setting the `downloadSdk` property to true makes it easy to run a local development server, because it automatically downloads the SDK if it is not present. If you already set up the Google App Engine SDK on your device, you can set the `downloadSdk` property to `false`.

The `appcfg` block is used to configure the App Engine SDK. In a typical Google App Engine installation, you can manually configure some settings by using the `appcfg` command-line tool. Using the `appcfg` block, instead of the command-line tool, makes the configuration a lot more portable, as anyone who ever builds the module will have the same configuration without needing to execute any external commands.

The endpoints block contains some Cloud Endpoints–specific settings.

 A detailed explanation of Google App Engine and Cloud Endpoints configurations is out of the scope of this book. If you wish to know more, look at the documentation at `https://cloud.google.com/appengine/docs`.

Using the backend in an app

When you create the App Engine module, Android Studio automatically adds a dependency to the build file of the Android app module. This dependency looks like this:

```
dependencies {
    compile project(path: ':backend', configuration: 'android-
        endpoints')
}
```

We saw syntax like this earlier (when referencing Java and Android libraries), using project to define the dependency, but with two parameters instead of just one. The path parameter is the default parameter. We used it earlier, but without specifying its name. A Google App Engine module can have different types of output. You can specify the output you want with the configuration parameter. We need the App Engine module to generate Cloud Endpoints, so we use the android-endpoints configuration. Internally, this configuration runs the _appengineEndpointsAndroidArtifact task. This task generates a JAR file that contains classes that you can use in your Android app module. This JAR file contains not only the models used in the Cloud Endpoints, but also API methods. Integration like this is what makes multimodule projects nice to work with because it speeds up development time. The Gradle tasks in the App Engine module also make it easy to run and deploy your backend.

Custom tasks

The App Engine plugin adds a lot of tasks, but the ones you will use the most are appengineRun and appengineUpdate.

The appengineRun task is used to start a local development server that you can use to test your entire backend locally before uploading it to Google App Engine. The first time you run this task, the build may take a while because Gradle needs to download the App Engine SDK. We set this behavior earlier with downloadSdk = true. To stop the server, you can use appengineStop.

Once you are ready to deploy your backend to Google App Engine and start using it in production, you can use appengineUpdate. This task handles all the deployment details. If you have set oauth2 = true in the appengine configuration block, this task will open a browser window, so you can log in to your Google account and get an authentication token. If you prefer not having to do this every time you need to deploy, you can log in to Android Studio with your Google account and use the IDE to deploy the backend. Android Studio runs the same Gradle task, but it will take care of the authentication for you.

Tips and best practices

There are a few ways to make it easier to deal with multimodule projects, and there are a few things to keep in mind when working with several modules. Being aware of these can save you time and frustration.

Running module tasks from Android Studio

As we saw in *Chapter 2, Basic Build Customization*, it is possible to run Gradle tasks straight from Android Studio. When you have multiple modules, Android Studio recognizes them, and shows a grouped overview of all available tasks.

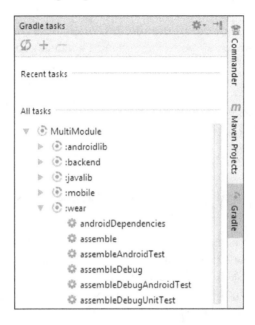

The Gradle tool window makes it easier to run module-specific tasks. There is no option to run a task for all modules at the same time, so if you wish to do that, the command-line interface is still faster.

Speeding up multimodule builds

When you build a multimodule project, Gradle processes all modules sequentially. With more and more cores available in computers, we can make the build process a lot faster by building the modules in parallel. This feature already exists in Gradle, but is not enabled by default.

If you want to apply parallel build execution to your project, you need to configure the `parallel` property in the `gradle.properties` file on the root of the project:

```
org.gradle.parallel=true
```

Gradle attempts to choose the right number of threads, based on available CPU cores. To prevent issues that may arise from executing two tasks from the same module in parallel, each thread *owns* an entire module.

 Parallel build execution is an incubating feature. This means that it is under active development and the implementation may change at any time. This feature has been a part of Gradle for a while now, though, and is already widely used. It is, therefore, safe to assume that the implementation will not disappear or change drastically.

Your mileage may vary, but you might be able to shave off a significant amount of time from your builds by simply enabling parallel build execution. There is one caveat, however. For this to work efficiently, you will need to make sure your modules are decoupled.

Module coupling

As we saw in *Chapter 2*, *Basic Build Customization*, it is possible to define properties for all modules in a project, using `allprojects` in the `build.gradle` file. When you have a project with multiple modules, you can use `allprojects` in any module to apply properties to all the modules in the project. Gradle even makes it possible for one module to reference properties from another module. These powerful features can make maintenance for multimodule builds a lot easier. The downside, though, is that your modules become coupled.

Two modules are considered to be coupled as soon as they access each other's tasks or properties. This has several consequences. For example, you give up portability. If you ever decide to extract a library out of the project, you will not be able to build the library before copying all project-wide settings first. Module coupling also has an effect on parallel builds. Using the `allprojects` block in any of the modules will render parallel build execution useless. Be aware of this when you add project-wide properties to any of the modules.

You can avoid coupling by not directly accessing tasks or properties from other modules. If you need this behavior, you can use the root module as an intermediary so that modules are coupled only to the root module and not to each other.

Summary

We started the chapter by looking at the structure of multimodule builds. Then, we looked at how to set up multiple modules in a single project. We also saw that adding new modules affects how build tasks are run.

We then looked at some practical examples of new modules, and how each of them can be integrated into a project. Finally, we mentioned some tips and tricks that make it easier to work with multiple modules in one project.

In the next chapter, we will set up various kinds of tests, and see how to use Gradle to make it easier to run these tests. We will look at running unit tests directly on the Java Virtual Machine, but also at running tests on a real device or an emulator.

6
Running Tests

To ensure the quality of any app or library, having automated tests is important. For a long time, the Android development tools lacked support for automated tests, but recently, Google has put in a lot of effort to make it easier for developers to get started with tests. Some old frameworks have been updated, and new frameworks have been added to make sure we can thoroughly test apps and libraries. We can run them not only from Android Studio, but also directly from the command-line interface, using Gradle.

In this chapter, we will explore the different ways to test Android apps and libraries. We will also look at how Gradle can help to automate the testing process.

We will cover the following topics in this chapter:

- Unit tests
- Functional tests
- Test coverage

Unit tests

Having well-written unit tests in your project does not only assure quality, it also makes it easy to check if new code breaks any functionality. Android Studio and the Gradle Android plugin have native support for unit tests, but you need to configure a few things before you can use them.

JUnit

JUnit is an extremely popular unit testing library that has been around for over a decade. It makes it easy to write tests while making sure that they are also easy to read. Keep in mind that these particular unit tests are only useful for testing business logic and not code that is related to the Android SDK.

Before you can start writing JUnit tests for your Android project, you need to create a directory for the tests. By convention, this directory is called `test` and it should be on the same level as your main directory. The directory structure should look like this:

```
app
└── src
    ├── main
    │   ├── java
    │   │   └── com.example.app
    │   └──res
    └── test
        └── java
            └── com.example.app
```

You can then create test classes in `src/test/java/com.example.app`.

To make use of the latest features in JUnit, use JUnit version 4. You can ensure this by adding a dependency for the test build:

```
dependencies {
    testCompile 'junit:junit:4.12'
}
```

Notice that we are using `testCompile` instead of `compile` here. We use this configuration to make sure that the dependency is only built when running the tests, and not when packaging the app for distribution. Dependencies added with `testCompile` will never be included in the APK releases generated by the regular assemble tasks.

If you have any special conditions in one of your build types or product flavors, it is possible to add a test-only dependency to that specific build alone. For example, if you only want to add JUnit tests to your paid flavor, you can do that as follows:

```
dependencies {
    testPaidCompile 'junit:junit:4.12'
}
```

When everything is set up, it is time to start writing some tests. Here is a simple example of a class that tests a method adding two numbers:

```
import org.junit.Test;

import static org.junit.Assert.assertEquals;

public class LogicTest {
    @Test
    public void addingNegativeNumberShouldSubtract() {
        Logic logic = new Logic();

        assertEquals("6 + -2 must be 4", 4, logic.add(6, -2));
        assertEquals("2 + -5 must be -3", -3, logic.add(2, -5));
    }
}
```

To run all tests with Gradle, just execute `gradlew` test. If you only want to run the tests on a certain build variant, simply add the name of the variant. If you want to run the tests on only the debug variant, for example, execute `gradlewtestDebug`. If a test fails, Gradle prints the error message in the command-line interface. If all the tests run smoothly, Gradle shows the regular **BUILD SUCCESSFUL** message.

A single failed test causes the `test` task to fail, halting the entire process immediately. This means that not all of your tests are executed in case of a failure. If you want to make sure the entire test suite is executed for all build variants, use the `continue` flag:

$ gradlew test --continue

You can also write tests specifically for a certain build variant by storing the tests class in the corresponding directory. For example, if you want to test specific behavior in the paid version of your app, put the test class in `src/testPaid/java/com.example.app`.

If you do not want to run the entire test suite, but only the tests for a particular class, you can use the tests flag like this:

$ gradlew testDebug --tests="*.LogicTest"

Executing the test task does not only run all the tests, but also creates a test report, which can be found at `app/build/reports/tests/debug/index.html`. This report makes it easy to find the issues if there are any failures, and is particularly useful in situations where tests are executed automatically. Gradle will create a report for every build variant that you run the tests on.

If all your tests run successfully, your unit test report will look like this:

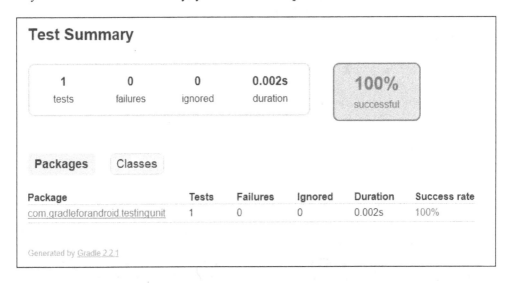

You can also run the tests within Android Studio. When you do that, you get immediate feedback in the IDE, and you can click on failed tests to navigate to the corresponding code. If all your tests pass, the **Run** tool window will look like this:

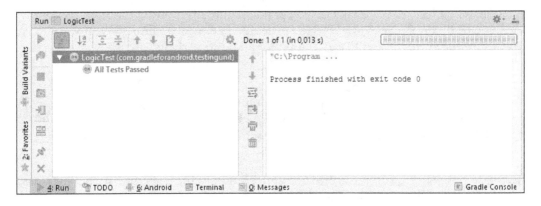

If you want to test parts of your code that contain references to Android-specific classes or resources, regular unit tests are not ideal. You may have already tried and run into the `java.lang.RuntimeException: Stub!` error. To fix this, you would need to implement every method in the Android SDK yourself, or use a mocking framework. Luckily, several libraries exist that have taken care of the Android SDK. The most popular of those libraries is Robolectric, which provides an easy way to test Android functionality, without the need for a device or emulator.

Robolectric

With Robolectric, you can write tests that make use of the Android SDK and resources, while still running tests inside the Java Virtual Machine. This means that you do not need a running device or emulator to make use of Android resources in your tests, thus making it a lot faster to test the behavior of UI components of an app or library.

To get started with Robolectric, you need to add a few test dependencies. Besides Robolectric itself, you also need to include JUnit, and, if you make use of the support library, you also need the Robolectric shadow classes to use it:

```
apply plugin: 'org.robolectric'
dependencies {
    compile fileTree(dir: 'libs', include: ['*.jar'])
    compile 'com.android.support:appcompat-v7:22.2.0'

    testCompile 'junit:junit:4.12'
    testCompile'org.robolectric:robolectric:3.0'
    testCompile'org.robolectric:shadows-support:3.0'
}
```

Robolectric tests classes should be created in the `src/test/java/com.example.app` directory, just like regular unit tests. The difference is that you can now write tests that involve Android classes and resources. For example, this test validates that the text of a certain `TextView` changes after clicking on a specific `Button`:

```
@RunWith(RobolectricTestRunner.class)
@Config(manifest = "app/src/main/AndroidManifest.xml", sdk = 18)
public class MainActivityTest {
    @Test
    public void clickingButtonShouldChangeText() {
        AppCompatActivity activity = Robolectric.buildActivity
            (MainActivity.class).create().get();
        Button button = (Button)
          activity.findViewById(R.id.button);
        TextView textView = (TextView)
          activity.findViewById(R.id.label);

        button.performClick();

        assertThat(textView.getText().toString(), equalTo
          (activity.getString(R.string.hello_robolectric)));
    }
}
```

Robolectric has some known issues with Android Lollipop and the compatibility library. If you run into errors that mention missing resources related to the compatibility library, there is a fix for that.

You need to add a file to the module called `project.properties`, and add these lines to it:

```
android.library.reference.1=../../build/intermediates/
exploded-aar/com.android.support/appcompat-v7/22.2.0
android.library.reference.2=../../build/intermediates/
exploded-aar/com.android.support/support-v4/22.2.0
```

This will help Robolectric find the compatibility library resources.

Functional tests

Functional tests are used to test whether several components of an app work together as expected. For example, you can create a functional test to confirm that tapping a certain button opens a new `Activity`. There are several functional testing frameworks for Android, but the easiest way to get started with functional testing is using the Espresso framework.

Espresso

Google created **Espresso** to make it easier for developers to write functional tests. The library is provided through the Android support repository, so you can install it using the SDK Manager.

In order to run tests on a device, you need to define a test runner. Through the testing support library, Google provides the `AndroidJUnitRunner` test runner, which helps you run JUnit test classes on Android devices. The test runner will load the app APK and the test APK to a device, run all the tests, and then build the reports with the test results.

Provided you have downloaded the testing support library, this is how you should set up the test runner:

```
defaultConfig {
    testInstrumentationRunner
        "android.support.test.runner.AndroidJUnitRunner"
}
```

You also need to set up a few dependencies before you can start using Espresso:

```
dependencies {
    compile fileTree(dir: 'libs', include: ['*.jar'])
    compile 'com.android.support:appcompat-v7:22.2.0'

    androidTestCompile 'com.android.support.test:runner:0.3'
    androidTestCompile 'com.android.support.test:rules:0.3'
    androidTestCompile
      'com.android.support.test.espresso:espresso-core:2.2'
    androidTestCompile
      'com.android.support.test.espresso:espresso-contrib:2.2'
}
```

You need to reference the testing support library and `espresso-core` to get started with Espresso. The last dependency, `espresso-contrib`, is a library with features that supplement Espresso, but are not part of the core library.

Notice that these dependencies use the `androidTestCompile` configuration, instead of the `testCompile` configuration we used earlier. This is to make a distinction between unit tests and functional tests.

If you were to try to run the test build at this point, you would run into this error:

```
Error: duplicate files during packaging of APK app-androidTest.apk
   Path in archive: LICENSE.txt
   Origin 1: ...\hamcrest-library-1.1.jar
   Origin 2: ...\junit-dep-4.10.jar
```

The error itself is very descriptive. Gradle cannot complete the build because of a duplicate file. Luckily, it is just a license description, so we can strip it out of the build. The error itself contains information on how to do that as well:

```
You can ignore those files in your build.gradle:
   android {
   packagingOptions {
       exclude 'LICENSE.txt'
     }
   }
```

Once the build file is set up, you can start adding tests. Functional tests are placed in a different directory than the regular unit tests. Just like with the dependency configurations, you need to use androidTest instead of just test, so the correct directory for functional tests is src/androidTest/java/com.example.app. Here is an example of a test class that checks whether the text of TextView in MainActivity is correct:

```
@RunWith(AndroidJUnit4.class)
@SmallTest
public class TestingEspressoMainActivityTest {
    @Rule
    public ActivityTestRule<MainActivity> mActivityRule = new
      ActivityTestRule<>(MainActivity.class);

    @Test
    public void testHelloWorldIsShown() {
        onView(withText("Hello world!")).check
          (matches(isDisplayed()));
    }
}
```

Before you can run Espresso tests, you need to make sure you have a device or emulator. If you forget to connect a device, trying to execute the test task will throw this exception:

```
Execution failed for task ':app:connectedAndroidTest'.
>com.android.builder.testing.api.DeviceException:
java.lang.RuntimeException: No connected devices!
```

Once you have connected a device or started an emulator, you can run your Espresso tests using gradlewconnectedCheck. This task will execute both connectedAndroidTest to run all tests for the debug build on all the connected devices, and createDebugCoverageReport to create a test report.

You can find the generated test reports in the app directory under build/outputs/ reports/androidTests/connected. Open index.html to view the report, which looks like this:

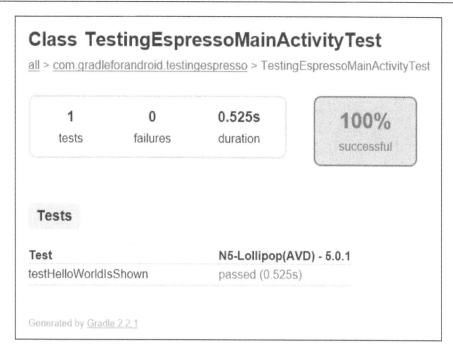

The functional test report shows which device and Android version the tests are run on. You can run these tests on multiple devices at the same time, so the device information makes it easier to find device- or version-specific bugs.

If you want to get feedback on your tests within Android Studio, set up a run/debug configuration to run the tests directly from the IDE. A run/debug configuration represents a set of run/debug startup properties. The Android Studio toolbar has a configuration picker, where you can select the run/debug configuration that you want to use.

To set up a new configuration, open the configuration editor by clicking on **Edit Configurations...** and then create a new Android tests configuration. Select the module and specify the instrumentation runner to be `AndroidJUnitRunner`, as shown in the following screenshot:

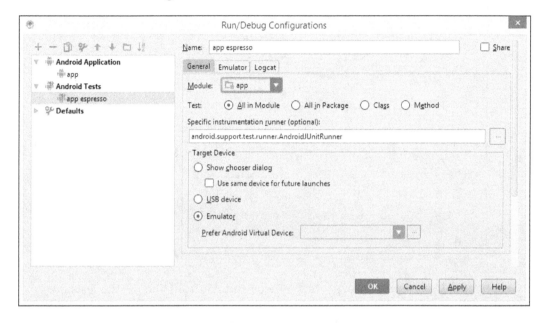

Once you save this new configuration, you can select it in the configuration picker and click on the **Run** button to run all tests.

 Running Espresso tests from Android Studio has one caveat: the test report is not generated. The reason for this is that Android Studio executes the `connectedAndroidTest` task instead of `connectedCheck`, and `connectedCheck` is the task that takes care of generating the test report.

Test coverage

Once you start writing tests for your Android projects, it is good to know how much of your code base is covered by tests. There are plenty of test coverage tools for Java, but **Jacoco** is the most popular one. It is also included by default, which makes it easy to get started.

Jacoco

Enabling coverage reports is very easy. You just need to set testCoverageEnabled = true on the build type that you are testing. Enable test coverage for the debug build type like this:

```
buildTypes {
  debug {
    testCoverageEnabled = true
  }
}
```

When you enable test coverage, the coverage reports are created when you execute gradlew connectedCheck. The task that creates the report itself is createDebugCoverageReport. Even though it is not documented, and it does not appear in the task list when you run gradlew tasks, it is possible to run it directly. However, because createCoverageReport depends on connectedCheck, you cannot execute them separately. The dependency on connectedCheck also means that you need a connected device or emulator to generate the test coverage report.

After the task is executed, you can find the coverage report in the app/build/outputs/reports/coverage/debug/index.html directory. Every build variant has its own directory for reports, because each variant can have different tests. The test coverage report will look something like this:

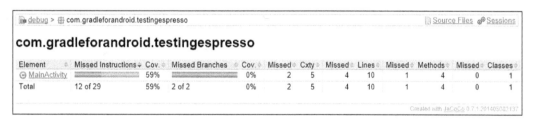

The report shows a nice overview of the coverage on the class level, and you can click through to get more information. In the most detailed view, you can see which lines are tested, and which ones are not, in a useful color-coded file view.

If you want to specify a particular version of Jacoco, simply add a Jacoco configuration block to the build type, defining the version:

```
jacoco {
  toolVersion = "0.7.1.201405082137"
}
```

However, explicitly defining a version is not necessary; Jacoco will work regardless.

Summary

In this chapter, we looked at several options to test Android apps and libraries. We started out with simple unit tests, and then looked at more Android-specific testing with Robolectric. Then we covered functional tests and getting started with Espresso. Finally, we looked at enabling test coverage reports to see where the test suite needs to be improved. Now that you know how to run the entire test suite with Gradle and Android Studio, and you can generate coverage reports, there are no excuses not to write tests. In *Chapter 8, Setting Up Continuous Integration*, we will look at more ways to automate tests with continuous integration tools.

The next chapter covers one of the most important aspects of customizing the build process: creating custom tasks and plugins. The chapter also includes a short introduction to Groovy. This will not only help when creating tasks and plugins, but will also make it easier to understand how Gradle works.

7
Creating Tasks and Plugins

So far, we have been manipulating properties for our Gradle builds and learning how to run tasks. In this chapter, we will get a deeper understanding of those properties, and start creating our own tasks. Once we know how to write our own tasks, we can go even further, and look at how to make our own plugins that can be reused in several projects.

Before we look at how to create custom tasks, we need to learn a few important Groovy concepts. This is because having a basic understanding of how Groovy works makes it a lot easier to get started with custom tasks and plugins. Knowing Groovy also helps to understand how Gradle works, and why the build configuration files look the way they do.

In this chapter, we will look at the following topics:

- Understanding Groovy
- Getting started with tasks
- Hooking into the Android plugin
- Creating your own plugins

Understanding Groovy

As most Android developers are proficient Java developers, it is interesting to look at how Groovy works compared to Java. Groovy is quite easy to read if you are a Java developer, but writing your own Groovy code would be a hard task without a small introduction.

A good way to experiment with Groovy is to use the Groovy Console. This application comes with the Groovy SDK and makes it easy to try out Groovy statements while getting an immediate response. The Groovy Console is also able to handle pure Java code, which makes it easy to compare Java and Groovy code. You can download the Groovy SDK, including the Groovy Console, from the Groovy website at `http://groovy-lang.org/download.html`.

Introduction

Groovy is derived from Java and runs on the Java Virtual Machine. Its goal is to be a simpler, more straightforward language that can be used either as a scripting language or as a full-blown programming language. Throughout this section, we will compare Groovy with Java to make it easier to grasp how Groovy works and to clearly see the difference between both languages.

In Java, printing a string to the screen looks like this:

```
System.out.println("Hello, world!");
```

In Groovy, you can accomplish the same with this line of code:

```
println 'Hello, world!'
```

You will immediately notice a few key differences:

- No `System.out` namespace
- No parentheses around method parameters
- No semicolons at the end of a line

The example also uses single quotes around a string. You can use either single quotes or double quotes for strings, but they have different usages. Double-quoted string can also include interpolated expressions. Interpolation is the process of evaluating a string that contains placeholders, and replacing those placeholders with their values. These placeholder expressions can be variables, or even methods. Placeholder expressions that contain a method or multiple variables need to be surrounded by curly brackets and prefixed by $. Placeholder expressions that contain a single variable can just be prefixed with $. Here are some examples of string interpolation in Groovy:

```
def name = 'Andy'
def greeting = "Hello, $name!"
def name_size "Your name is ${name.size()} characters long."
```

The `greeting` variable contains the string "Hello, Andy" and `name_size` is "Your name is 4 characters long.".

String interpolation allows you to execute code dynamically as well. This example is valid code that prints the current date:

```
def method = 'toString'
new Date()."$method"()
```

This looks very strange when you are used to Java, but it is normal syntax and behavior in dynamic programming languages.

Classes and members

Creating a class in Groovy looks a lot like creating a class in Java. Here is an example of a simple class containing one member:

```
class MyGroovyClass {
    String greeting

    String getGreeting() {
        return 'Hello!'
    }
}
```

Notice that neither the class nor the member has explicit access modifiers. The default access modifiers in Groovy are different from in Java. Classes themselves are public, just like methods, while class members are private.

To use `MyGroovyClass`, make a new instance of it:

```
def instance = new MyGroovyClass()
instance.setGreeting 'Hello, Groovy!'
instance.getGreeting()
```

You can use the keyword `def` to create new variables. Once you have a new instance of a class, you can manipulate its members. Accessors are added automatically by Groovy. You can still override them, as we did with `getGreeting()` in the definition of `MyGroovyClass`. If you specify nothing, you will still be able to use both a getter and a setter for every member in your class.

If you try to call a member directly, you will, in fact, call the getter. This means you do not need to type `instance.getGreeting()`, you can just use the shorter `instance.greeting` instead:

```
println instance.getGreeting()
println instance.greeting
```

Both lines in the preceding code sample print out the exact same thing.

Methods

Just like with variables, you do not need to define a specific return type for your methods. You are free to do so anyway, even if it is just for the sake of clarity. Another difference between Java and Groovy methods is that in Groovy, the last line of a method is always returned by default, even without using the `return` keyword.

To demonstrate the differences between Java and Groovy, consider this Java example of a method that returns the square of a number:

```
public int square(int num) {
    return num * num;
}
square(2);
```

You need to specify that the method is publicly accessible, what the return type is, and what the type of the parameter is. At the end of the method, you need to return a value of the return type.

The same method definition looks like this in Groovy:

```
def square(def num) {
    num * num
}
square 4
```

Neither the return type, nor the parameter type is explicitly defined. The `def` keyword is used instead of an explicit type, and the method implicitly returns a value without using the `return` keyword. However, using the `return` keyword is still recommended for clarity. When you call the method, you do not need parentheses or semicolon.

There is also another, even shorter, way to define new methods in Groovy. The same `square` method can also look like this:

```
def square = { num ->
    num * num
}
square 8
```

This is not a regular method, but a closure. The concept of closures does not exist in the same way in Java, but it plays a significant role in Groovy and in Gradle especially.

Closures

Closures are anonymous blocks of code that can accept parameters and can return a value. They can be assigned to variables and can be passed as parameters to methods.

You can define a closure simply by adding a block of code between curly brackets, as you saw in the previous example. If you want to be a bit more explicit, you can add the type to your definition, like this:

```
Closure square = {
    it * it
}
square 16
```

Adding the `Closure` type makes it clear to everyone working with the code that a closure is being defined. The preceding example also introduces the concept of an implicit untyped argument named `it`. If you do not explicitly add a parameter to a closure, Groovy will add one automatically. This parameter is always called `it`, and you can use it in all closures. If the caller does not specify any parameters, `it` is null. This can make your code a bit more concise, but it is only useful if the closure takes just one single parameter.

In the context of Gradle, we work with closures all the time. In this book, we have been referring to closures as blocks so far. This means that, for example, the `android` block and the `dependencies` block are closures.

Collections

There are two important collection types when using Groovy in a Gradle context: lists and maps.

Creating a new list in Groovy is easy. There is no need for special initializers; you can simply create a list like this:

```
List list = [1, 2, 3, 4, 5]
```

Iterating over a list is also extremely easy. You can use the `each` method to iterate over every element in a list:

```
list.each() { element ->
    println element
}
```

The `each` method enables you to access each element in the list. You can make this code even shorter by using the `it` variable that was mentioned earlier:

```
list.each() {
    println it
}
```

Another type of collection that is important in the context of Gradle is `Map`. Maps are used in several Gradle settings and methods. A map is, simply put, a list that contains key-value pairs. You can define a map like this:

```
Map pizzaPrices = [margherita:10, pepperoni:12]
```

To access specific items in a map, use the `get` method or square brackets:

```
pizzaPrices.get('pepperoni')
pizzaPrices['pepperoni']
```

Groovy has a shortcut for this functionality as well. You can use dot notation for map elements, using the key to retrieve the value:

```
pizzaPrices.pepperoni
```

Groovy in Gradle

Now that you know the basics of Groovy, it is an interesting exercise to go back, look at a Gradle build file, and read it. Notice that it has become easier to understand why the syntax for configuration looks the way it does. For example, look at the line where the Android plugin is applied to the build:

```
apply plugin: 'com.android.application'
```

This piece of code is full of Groovy shortcuts. If you write it out without any of the shortcuts, it looks like this:

```
project.apply([plugin: 'com.android.application'])
```

Rewriting the line without Groovy shortcuts makes it clear that `apply()` is a method of the `Project` class, which is the basic building block of every Gradle build. The `apply()` method takes one parameter, which is a `Map` with a key `plugin` and value `com.android.application`.

Another example is the `dependencies` block. Previously, we defined dependencies like this:

```
dependencies {
    compile 'com.google.code.gson:gson:2.3'
}
```

We now know that this block is a closure, passed to the dependencies() method on a Project object. This closure is passed to a DependencyHandler, which contains the add() method. That method accepts three parameters: a string defining the configuration, an object defining the dependency notation, and a closure that contains properties specifically for this dependency. When you write this out in full, it looks like this:

```
project.dependencies({
    add('compile', 'com.google.code.gson:gson:2.3', {
        // Configuration statements
    })
})
```

The build configuration files we have been looking at so far should start making a lot more sense, now that you know what it looks like behind the curtains.

 If you want to know more about the way Gradle makes use of Groovy under the hood, you can use the official documentation for Project as a starting point. You can find it at http://gradle.org/docs/current/javadoc/org/gradle/api/Project.html.

Getting started with tasks

Custom Gradle tasks can significantly improve the daily life of a developer. Tasks can manipulate the existing build process, add new build steps, or influence the outputs of a build. You can perform simple tasks, such as renaming a generated APK, by hooking into the Android plugin for Gradle. Tasks also enable you to run more complex code, so you can generate images for several densities before your app is packaged, for instance. Once you know how to create your own tasks, you will find yourself empowered to change every aspect of your build process. This is especially true when you learn how to hook into the Android plugin.

Defining tasks

Tasks belong to a Project object, and each task implements the Task interface. The easiest way to define a new task is by executing the task method with the name of the task as its parameter:

```
task hello
```

This creates the task, but it will not do anything when you execute it. To create a task that is somewhat useful, you need to add some actions to it. A common beginner's mistake is to create tasks like this:

```
task hello {
    println 'Hello, world!'
}
```

When you execute this task, you see this output:

```
$ gradlew hello
Hello, world!
:hello
```

From the output, you might get the impression that this works, but, in fact, "Hello, world!" was printed out before the task was even executed. To understand what is going on here, we need to get back to the basics. In *Chapter 1, Getting Started with Gradle and Android Studio*, we talked about the lifecycle of a Gradle build. There are three phases in any Gradle build: the initialization phase, the configuration phase, and the execution phase. When you add code to a task in the same way as in the previous example, you are actually setting up the configuration of the task. Even if you were to execute a different task, the "Hello, world!" message would still show up.

If you want to add actions to a task for the execution phase, use this notation:

```
task hello << {
    println 'Hello, world!'
}
```

The only difference here is the << before the closure. This tells Gradle that the code is meant for the execution phase, and not the configuration phase.

To demonstrate the difference, consider this build file:

```
task hello << {
    println 'Execution'
}

hello {
    println 'Configuration'
}
```

We define the task `hello`, which prints to the screen when it is executed. We also define code for the configuration phase of the `hello` task, which prints `Configuration` to the screen. Even though the configuration block is defined after the actual task code definition, it will still be executed first. This is the output of the preceding example:

```
$ gradlew hello
Configuration
:hello
Execution
```

> Accidental use of the configuration phase resulting in failing tasks is a common mistake. Keep that in mind when you start creating your own tasks.

Because Groovy has so many shortcuts, there are several ways to define tasks in Gradle:

```
task(hello) << {
    println 'Hello, world!'
}

task('hello') << {
    println 'Hello, world!'
}

tasks.create(name: 'hello') << {
    println 'Hello, world!'
}
```

The first two blocks are just two different ways to achieve the same thing with Groovy. You can use parentheses, but you do not need to. You do not need single quotes around the parameter either. In these two blocks, we call the `task()` method, which takes in two parameters: a string for the name of the task, and a closure. The `task()` method is a part of Gradle's `Project` class.

The last block does not use the `task()` method. Instead, it makes use of an object named `tasks`, which is an instance of `TaskContainer`, and is present in every `Project` object. This class provides a `create()` method that takes a `Map` and a closure as parameters and returns a `Task`.

It is convenient to write the short form, and most online examples and tutorials will use them. However, writing the longer form can be useful while learning. This way, Gradle will seem a lot less like magic, and it will become a lot easier to understand what is going on.

Anatomy of a task

The `Task` interface is the basis of all tasks and defines a collection of properties and methods. All of these are implemented by a class named `DefaultTask`. This is the standard task type implementation, and when you create a new task, it is based on `DefaultTask`.

 Technically speaking, `DefaultTask` is not really the class that implements all the methods in the `Task` interface. Gradle has an internal type named `AbstractTask`, that contains the implementation for all the methods. Because `AbstractTask` is internal, we cannot override it. Thus, we focus on `DefaultTask`, which derives from `AbstractTask`, and which can be overridden.

Every `Task` contains a collection of `Action` objects. When a task is executed, all of these actions are executed in a sequential order. To add actions to a task, you can use the methods `doFirst()` and `doLast()`. These methods both take a closure as a parameter, and then wrap it into an `Action` object for you.

You always need to use either `doFirst()` or `doLast()` to add code to a task if you want that code to be a part of the execution phase. The left-shift operator (<<) we used previously to define tasks is a shortcut for the `doFirst()` method.

Here is an example of the use of `doFirst()` and `doLast()`:

```
task hello {
  println 'Configuration'

  doLast {
    println 'Goodbye'
  }

  doFirst {
    println 'Hello'
  }
}
```

When you execute the `hello` task, this is the output:

```
$ gradlew hello
Configuration
:hello
Hello
Goodbye
```

Even though the line of code that prints "Goodbye" is defined before the line of code that prints "Hello", they end up in the correct order when the task is executed. You can even use `doFirst()` and `doLast()` multiple times, as shown in this example:

```
task mindTheOrder {
  doFirst {
    println 'Not really first.'
  }

  doFirst {
    println 'First!'
  }

  doLast {
    println 'Not really last.'
  }

  doLast {
    println 'Last!'
  }
}
```

Executing this task will return the following output:

```
$ gradlew mindTheOrder
:mindTheOrder
First!
Not really first.
Not really last.
Last!
```

Notice how `doFirst()` always adds an action to the very beginning of a task, and `doLast()` adds an action to the very end. This means you need to be careful when you use these methods, especially when the order is important.

When it comes to ordering tasks, you can use the `mustRunAfter()` method. This method allows you to influence how Gradle constructs the dependency graph. When you use `mustRunAfter()`, you specify that if two tasks are executed, one must always be executed before the other:

```
task task1 << {
    println 'task1'
}
task task2 << {
    println 'task2'
}
task2.mustRunAfter task1
```

Running both `task1` and `task2` will always result in the execution of `task1` before `task2`, regardless of the order you specify:

```
$ gradlew task2 task1
:task1
task1
:task2
task2
```

The `mustRunAfter()` method does not add a dependency between the tasks; it is still possible to execute `task2` without executing `task1`. If you need one task to depend on another, use the `dependsOn()` method instead. The difference between `mustRunAfter()` and `dependsOn()` is best explained with an example:

```
task task1 << {
    println 'task1'
}
task task2 << {
    println 'task2'
}
task2.dependsOn task1
```

This is what it looks like when you try to execute `task2` without executing `task1`:

```
$ gradlew task2
:task1
task1
:task2
task2
```

Using `mustRunAfter()`, `task1` is always executed before `task2` when you run them both, but both can still be executed independently. With `dependsOn()`, the execution of `task2` always triggers `task1` as well, even if it is not explicitly mentioned. This is an important distinction.

Using a task to simplify the release process

Before you can release an Android app to the Google Play store, you need to sign it with a certificate. To do this, you need to create your own keystore, which contains a set of private keys. When you have your keystore and a private key for the application, you can define the signing configuration in Gradle, like this:

```
android {
    signingConfigs {
        release {
```

```
            storeFile file("release.keystore")
            storePassword "password"
            keyAlias "ReleaseKey"
            keyPassword "password"
        }
    }

    buildTypes {
        release {
            signingConfig signingConfigs.release
        }
    }
}
```

The downside of this approach is that your keystore passwords are stored in plaintext in the repository. If you are working on an open source project, this is a definite no-go; anyone with access to both the keystore file and the keystore passwords would be able to publish apps using your identity. In order to prevent this, you could create a task that asks for the release passwords every time you assemble the release package. This is a little cumbersome though, and it makes it impossible for your build server to automatically generate release builds. A good solution to store the keystore passwords is to create a configuration file that is not included in the repository.

Start by creating a file named `private.properties` in the root of the project, and add this line to it:

```
release.password = thepassword
```

We assume that the passwords for both the keystore and the key itself are the same. If you have two different passwords, it is easy to add a second property.

Once that is set up, you can define a new task named `getReleasePassword`:

```
task getReleasePassword << {
    def password = ''

    if (rootProject.file('private.properties').exists()) {
        Properties properties = new Properties();
        properties.load( rootProject.file
          ('private.properties').newDataInputStream())
        password = properties.getProperty('release.password')
    }
}
```

This task will look for a file named `private.properties` in the root of the project. If this file exists, the task will load all properties from its content. The `properties.load()` method looks for key-value pairs, such as the `release.password` we defined in the properties file.

To make sure anyone can run the script without the private properties files, or to handle the case where the properties file exists, but the password property is not present, add a fallback. If the password is still empty, ask for the password in the console:

```
if (!password?.trim()) {
    password = new String(System.console().readPassword
        ("\nWhat's the secret password? "))
}
```

Checking if a string is not null or empty is a very concise process with Groovy. The question mark in `password?.trim()` does a null check and will prevent the `trim()` method from being called if it turns out `password` is null. We do not need to explicitly check for null or empty, because both null and empty strings are equal to false in the context of an if-clause.

The use of `new String()` is necessary because `System.readPassword()` returns an array of characters, which needs to be converted to a string explicitly.

Once we have the keystore passwords, we can configure the signing configuration for the release build:

```
android.signingConfigs.release.storePassword = password
android.signingConfigs.release.keyPassword = password
```

Now that we have finished our task, we need to make sure it is executed when performing a release build. To do this, add these lines to the `build.gradle` file:

```
tasks.whenTaskAdded { theTask ->
    if (theTask.name.equals("packageRelease")) {
        theTask.dependsOn "getReleasePassword"
    }
}
```

This code hooks into Gradle and the Android plugin by adding a closure that needs to be run when the tasks are being added to the dependency graph. The password is not required until the `packageRelease` task is executed, so we make sure that `packageRelease` depends on our `getReleasePassword` task. The reason we cannot just use `packageRelease.dependsOn()` is that the Android plugin for Gradle generates the packaging tasks dynamically, based on the build variants. This means that the `packageRelease` task does not exist until the Android plugin has discovered all of the build variants. The discovery process is kicked off before every single build.

After adding the task and the build hook, this is the result of executing `gradlew assembleRelease`:

```
:GradleForAndroid:compileReleaseAidl UP-TO-DATE
:GradleForAndroid:compileReleaseRenderscript UP-TO-DATE
:GradleForAndroid:generateReleaseBuildConfig UP-TO-DATE
:GradleForAndroid:generateReleaseAssets UP-TO-DATE
:GradleForAndroid:mergeReleaseAssets UP-TO-DATE
:GradleForAndroid:generateReleaseResValues UP-TO-DATE
:GradleForAndroid:generateReleaseResources UP-TO-DATE
:GradleForAndroid:mergeReleaseResources UP-TO-DATE
:GradleForAndroid:processReleaseManifest UP-TO-DATE
:GradleForAndroid:crashlyticsGenerateResourcesRelease
:GradleForAndroid:processReleaseResources
:GradleForAndroid:generateReleaseSources
:GradleForAndroid:compileReleaseJava UP-TO-DATE
:GradleForAndroid:proguardRelease UP-TO-DATE
:GradleForAndroid:dexRelease UP-TO-DATE
:GradleForAndroid:crashlyticsStoreDeobsRelease
:GradleForAndroid:crashlyticsUploadDeobsRelease
:GradleForAndroid:lintVitalRelease
:GradleForAndroid:compileReleaseNdk UP-TO-DATE
:GradleForAndroid:getReleasePassword
If you want to make it easier on yourself, create a file called private.properties in the root of the
roject and add "release.password = [password]" to it. Then the script will read that property instead
f asking for the password every time.
> Building 87% > :GradleForAndroid:getReleasePasswordWhat's the secret password?
:GradleForAndroid:processReleaseJavaRes UP-TO-DATE
:GradleForAndroid:validateReleaseSigning
:GradleForAndroid:packageRelease
:GradleForAndroid:zipalignRelease
:GradleForAndroid:assembleRelease

BUILD SUCCESSFUL

Total time: 22.926 secs
```

As you can see in the preceding screenshot, the `private.properties` file was not available, so the task asked for the password in the console. In this case, we also added a message explaining how to create the properties file and add the password property to make future builds easier. Once our task picked up the keystore password, Gradle was able to package our app and finish the build.

To get this task to work, it was essential to hook into Gradle and the Android plugin. This is a powerful concept, so we will explore this in detail.

Hooking into the Android plugin

When developing for Android, most tasks we want to influence are related to the Android plugin. It is possible to augment the behavior of tasks by hooking into the build process. In the previous example, we already saw how to add a dependency on a custom task to include a new task in the regular build process. In this section, we will look at some possibilities for Android-specific build hooks.

One way to hook into the Android plugin is to manipulate the build variants. Doing this is quite straightforward; you just need the following code snippet to iterate over all the build variants of an app:

```
android.applicationVariants.all { variant ->
  // Do something
}
```

To get the collection of build variants, you can use the `applicationVariants` object. Once you have a reference to a build variant, you can access and manipulate its properties, such as name, description, and so on. If you want to use the same logic for an Android library, use `libraryVariants` instead of `applicationVariants`.

> Notice that we iterate over the build variants with `all()` instead of the `each()` method that we mentioned earlier. This is necessary because `each()` is triggered in the evaluation phase before the build variants have been created by the Android plugin. The `all()` method, on the other hand, is triggered every time a new item is added to the collection.

This hook can be used to change the name of the APK before it is saved, to add the version number to the filename. This makes it easy to maintain an archive of APKs without manually editing file names. In the next section, we will see how to accomplish that.

Automatically renaming APKs

A common use case for manipulating the build process is to rename APKs to include the version number after they are packaged. You can do this by iterating over the build variants of the app, and changing the `outputFile` property of its outputs, as demonstrated in the following code snippet:

```
android.applicationVariants.all { variant ->
  variant.outputs.each { output ->
    def file = output.outputFile
```

```
output.outputFile = new File(file.parent,
    file.name.replace(".apk", "-${variant.versionName}.apk"))
}
}
```

Every build variant has a collection of outputs. The output of an Android app is just an APK. The output objects each have a property of the type `File` named `outputFile`. Once you know the path of the output, you can manipulate it. In this example, we add the version name of the variant to the file name. This will result in an APK named `app-debug-1.0.apk` instead of `app-debug.apk`.

Combining the power of build hooks for the Android plugin with the simplicity of Gradle tasks opens up a world of possibilities. In the next section, we will see how to create a task for every build variant of an app.

Dynamically creating new tasks

Because of the way that Gradle works and tasks are constructed, we can easily create our own tasks in the configuration phase, based on the Android build variants. To demonstrate this powerful concept, we will create a task to not just install, but also run any build variant of an Android app. The `install` task is a part of the Android plugin, but if you install an app from the command-line interface using the `installDebug` task, you will still need to start it manually when the installation is complete. The task we will create in this section will eliminate that last step.

Start by hooking into the `applicationVariants` property that we used earlier:

```
android.applicationVariants.all { variant ->
  if (variant.install) {
    tasks.create(name: "run${variant.name.capitalize()}",
      dependsOn: variant.install) {
        description "Installs the ${variant.description} and runs
          the main launcher activity."
    }
  }
}
```

For every variant, we check if it has a valid `install` task. This needs to be present because the new `run` task we are creating will depend on the `install` task. Once we have verified that the `install` task is present, we create a new task, and name it based on the variant's name. We also make our new task dependent on `variant.install`. This will trigger the `install` task before our task is executed. Inside the `tasks.create()` closure, start by adding a description, which is displayed when you execute `gradlew tasks`.

Besides adding the description, we also need to add the actual task action. In this example, we want to launch the app. You can launch an app on a connected device or emulator with the **Android Debug Tool (ADB)**:

```
$ adb shell am start -n com.package.name/com.package.name.Activity
```

Gradle has a method called `exec()` that makes it possible to execute a command-line process. To make `exec()` work, we need to provide an executable that is present in the `PATH` environment variable. We also need to pass all the parameters with the `args` property, which takes a list of strings. Here is what that looks like:

```
doFirst {
    exec {
        executable = 'adb'
        args = ['shell', 'am', 'start', '-n',
          "${variant.applicationId}/.MainActivity"]
    }
}
```

To get the full package name, use the application ID of the build variant, which includes a suffix, if provided. There is one issue with suffixes in this case, though. Even if we add a suffix, the classpath to the activity is still the same. For example, consider this configuration:

```
android {
    defaultConfig {
        applicationId 'com.gradleforandroid'
    }

    buildTypes {
        debug {
            applicationIdSuffix '.debug'
        }
    }
}
```

The package name is `com.gradleforandroid.debug`, but the activity's path is still `com.gradleforandroid.Activity`. To make sure we get the right class to the activity, strip the suffix from the application ID:

```
doFirst {
    def classpath = variant.applicationId
    if(variant.buildType.applicationIdSuffix) {
        classpath -= "${variant.buildType.applicationIdSuffix}"
    }
    def launchClass =
      "${variant.applicationId}/${classpath}.MainActivity"
```

```
exec {
    executable = 'adb'
    args = ['shell', 'am', 'start', '-n', launchClass]
}
}
```

First, we create a variable named `classpath`, based on the application ID. Then we find the suffix, provided by the `buildType.applicationIdSuffix` property. In Groovy, it is possible to subtract a string from another string, using the minus operator. These changes make sure running the app after installation does not fail when suffixes are used.

Creating your own plugins

If you have a collection of Gradle tasks that you want to reuse in several projects, it makes sense to extract these tasks into a custom plugin. This makes it possible to reuse build logic yourself, and to share it with others.

Plugins can be written in Groovy, but also in other languages that make use of the JVM, such as Java and Scala. In fact, big parts of the Android plugin for Gradle are written in Java in combination with Groovy.

Creating a simple plugin

To extract build logic that is already stored in your build configuration file, you can create a plugin within the `build.gradle` file. This is the easiest way to get started with custom plugins.

To create a plugin, create a new class that implements the `Plugin` interface. We will use the code we wrote previously in this chapter, which dynamically creates `run` tasks. Our plugin class looks like this:

```
class RunPlugin implements Plugin<Project> {
  void apply(Project project) {
    project.android.applicationVariants.all { variant ->
      if (variant.install) {
        project.tasks.create(name:
          "run${variant.name.capitalize()}",
          dependsOn: variant.install) {
            // Task definition
        }
      }
    }
  }
}
```

The `Plugin` interface defines an `apply()` method. Gradle calls this method when the plugin is used in a build file. The project is passed as a parameter so that the plugin can configure the project or use its methods and properties. In the preceding example, we cannot call properties from the Android plugin directly. Instead, we need to access the project object first. Note that this requires the Android plugin to be applied to the project before our custom plugin is applied. Otherwise, `project.android` will cause an exception.

The code for the task is the same as it was earlier, except for one method call: instead of calling `exec()`, we now need to call `project.exec()`.

To make sure the plugin is applied to our build configuration, add this line to `build.gradle`:

```
apply plugin: RunPlugin
```

Distributing plugins

In order to distribute a plugin and share it with others, you need to move it into a standalone module (or project). A standalone plugin has its own build file to configure dependencies and means of distribution. This module produces a JAR file, containing the plugin classes and properties. You can use this JAR file to apply the plugin in several modules and projects, and to share it with others.

As with any Gradle project, create a `build.gradle` file to configure the build:

```
apply plugin: 'groovy'

dependencies {
    compile gradleApi()
    compile localGroovy()
}
```

Since we are writing the plugin in Groovy, we need to apply the Groovy plugin. The Groovy plugin extends on the Java plugin, and enables us to build and package Groovy classes. Both Groovy and plain Java are supported, so you can mix them if you like. You can even go so far as to extend a Java class using Groovy, or the other way around. This makes it easy to get started, even if you do not feel confident using Groovy for everything.

Our build configuration file contains two dependencies: `gradleApi()` and `localGroovy()`. The Gradle API is required to access Gradle namespaces from our custom plugin, and `localGroovy()` is a distribution of the Groovy SDK that comes with the Gradle installation. Gradle provides these dependencies by default for our convenience. If Gradle did not provide these dependencies out of the box, we would have to download and reference them manually.

> If you plan to distribute your plugin publically, make sure to specify the group and version information in the build configuration file, like this:
> ```
> group = 'com.gradleforandroid'
> version = '1.0'
> ```

To get started with the code in our standalone module, we first need to make sure to use the correct directory structure:

```
plugin
└── src
    └── main
        ├── groovy
        │   └── com
        │       └── package
        │           └── name
        └── resources
            └── META-INF
                └── gradle-plugins
```

As with any other Gradle module, we need to provide a `src/main` directory. Because this is a Groovy project, the subdirectory of `main` is called `groovy` instead of `java`. There is another subdirectory of `main` called `resources`, which we will use to specify our plugin's properties.

We create a file called `RunPlugin.groovy` in the package directory, where we define the class for our plugin:

```
package com.gradleforandroid

import org.gradle.api.Project
import org.gradle.api.Plugin

class RunPlugin implements Plugin<Project> {
    void apply(Project project) {
        project.android.applicationVariants.all { variant ->
            // Task code
        }
    }
}
```

In order for Gradle to be able to find the plugin, we need to provide a properties file. Add this properties file to the `src/main/resources/META-INF/gradle-plugins/` directory. The name of the file needs to match the ID of our plugin. For the `RunPlugin`, the file is named `com.gradleforandroid.run.properties`, and this is its content:

```
implementation-class=com.gradleforandroid.RunPlugin
```

The only thing that the properties file contains is the package and name of the class that implements the `Plugin` interface.

When the plugin and the properties file are ready, we can build the plugin using the `gradlew assemble` command. This creates a JAR file in the build output directory. If you want to push the plugin to a Maven repository instead, you first need to apply the Maven plugin:

```
apply plugin: 'maven'
```

Next, you need to configure the `uploadArchives` task, like this:

```
uploadArchives {
    repositories {
        mavenDeployer {
            repository(url: uri('repository_url'))
    }
        }
    }
```

The `uploadArchives` task is a predefined task. Once you configure a repository on the task, you can execute it to publish your plugin. We will not cover how to set up a Maven repository in this book.

If you want to make your plugin publically available, consider publishing it to Gradleware's plugin portal (`https://plugins.gradle.org`). The plugin portal has a great collection of Gradle plugins (not just specific to Android development) and is the place to go when you want to extend Gradle's default behavior. You can find information on how to publish a plugin in the documentation at `https://plugins.gradle.org/docs/submit`.

 Writing tests for custom plugins is not covered in this book, but is highly recommended if you plan to make your plugins publically available. You can find more information on writing tests for plugins in the Gradle user guide at `https://gradle.org/docs/current/userguide/custom_plugins.html#N16CE1`.

Using a custom plugin

To use a plugin, we need to add it as a dependency to the `buildscript` block. First, we need to configure a new repository. The configuration of the repository depends on the way that the plugin is distributed. Second, we need to configure the classpath of the plugin in the `dependencies` block.

If we want to include the JAR file that we created in the earlier example, we can define a `flatDir` repository:

```
buildscript {
    repositories {
        flatDir { dirs 'build_libs' }
    }
    dependencies {
        classpath 'com.gradleforandroid:plugin'
    }
}
```

If we had uploaded the plugin to a Maven or Ivy repository, this would look a little different. We covered dependency management already in *Chapter 3, Managing Dependencies*, so we will not repeat the different options here.

After we set up the dependency, we need to apply the plugin:

```
apply plugin: com.gradleforandroid.RunPlugin
```

When using the `apply()` method, Gradle creates an instance of the plugin class, and executes the plugin's own `apply()` method.

Summary

In this chapter, we discovered how Groovy is different from Java, and how Groovy is used in Gradle. We saw how to create our own tasks and how to hook into the Android plugin, giving us a lot of power to manipulate the build process or dynamically add our own tasks.

In the last part of the chapter, we looked at creating plugins and ensured that we can reuse them in several projects by creating a standalone plugin. There is much more to learn about plugins, but unfortunately, we cannot cover it all in this book. Luckily, the Gradle user guide has a thorough description of all the possibilities at `https://gradle.org/docs/current/userguide/custom_plugins.html`.

In the next chapter, we will talk about the importance of continuous integration (CI). With a good CI system in place, we can build, test, and deploy apps and libraries with one click. Continuous integration is thus an important part of build automation in general.

8
Setting Up Continuous Integration

Continuous integration (**CI**) is a development practice that requires the developers in a team to integrate their work regularly, often multiple times per day. Every push to the main repository is verified by an automated build. This practice helps with detecting problems as soon as possible, thereby speeding up development, and increasing the quality of the code. The great Martin Fowler wrote an article about the subject that explains the concepts and describes the best practices (`http://martinfowler.com/articles/continuousIntegration.html`)

There are several options to set up CI for Android. The most widely used are **Jenkins**, **TeamCity**, and **Travis CI**. Jenkins has the biggest ecosystem, with around a thousand available plugins. It is also an open source effort with a lot of contributors. TeamCity is a product from JetBrains, the company that also created IntelliJ IDEA. Travis CI is a relatively new player, and is mostly focused on open source projects.

We will look at these CI systems and how to make Gradle work on them. At the end of the chapter, we will mention some Gradle tricks to make CI easier, regardless of the chosen CI system.

In this chapter, we will cover the following topics:

- Jenkins
- TeamCity
- Travis CI
- Further automation

Jenkins

Jenkins was originally released as Hudson in 2005 by Sun Microsystems. Over the years, it grew to become the most popular CI system in the Java community. Shortly after Sun Microsystems was acquired by Oracle, there was a conflict between Oracle and the Java community regarding Hudson. When that could not be resolved, the community continued to work on the project under the name Jenkins because the name Hudson is owned by Oracle.

The power of Jenkins lies in its plugin system. Everyone who has a need for new functionality in the build system can create a new plugin that extends the capabilities of Jenkins. This is also why setting up an automated build for Android apps or libraries is quite straightforward.

Setting up Jenkins

If you do not already have Jenkins installed and running on your build machine, download it from the website (`https://jenkins-ci.org`) and follow the steps.

Before you can get started with the actual Jenkins setup, you need to make sure you have all the required libraries for building Android apps and libraries. To build anything in Java, you need to download and install the JDK first, which can be downloaded from the Java website (`http://www.oracle.com/technetwork/java/javase/downloads/index.html`).

You also need to make sure you have the Android SDK and build tools installed. It is not necessary to install an IDE on your build server, unless you plan on opening the project on the build machine. If you just want to install the SDK tools, you can download those from the Android developer website (`https://developer.android.com/sdk/index.html#Other`). Once you have downloaded and installed the package, you need to run the `android` executable in the SDK directory, so you can install the APIs and build tools you need.

Once Java and the Android SDK are installed, you need to configure these in Jenkins. Start by opening your web browser and navigating to Jenkins' home page on your build server. Go to **Manage Jenkins | Configure System** and scroll to **Global properties**. Add two environment variables, `ANDROID_HOME` and `JAVA_HOME`, and set their values to the correct directories, as shown in this screenshot:

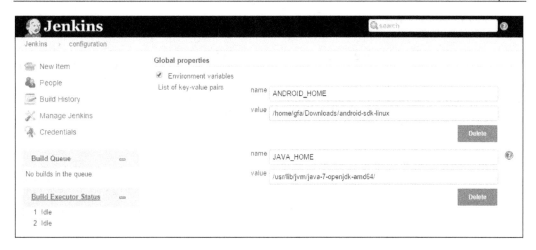

You also need to install the Gradle plugin. Go to **Manage Jenkins | Manage Plugins**, navigate to the **Available** tab, and search for `Gradle`. When you locate the Gradle plugin, simply check the box and click on **Download now and install after restart**. This plugin makes it possible to create build steps that involve Gradle.

Configuring the build

Once you have installed everything you need, you can create a CI project in Jenkins. The first thing you should do is to set up the VCS repository, so that Jenkins knows where to get the source code for your project. You can set up Jenkins to build your app or library automatically based on repository activity, using build triggers, or you can choose to only do manual builds. To perform the actual build, you need to add a new build step that invokes a Gradle script. You can configure Jenkins to use the Gradle Wrapper, which is present by default in Android projects. Using the Gradle Wrapper not only eliminates the need for manually installing Gradle on your build server, it also makes sure that any updates of Gradle are handled automatically. It is a good idea to also check the **Make gradlew executable** box. This solves an issue with permission for executing the Gradle Wrapper, when the project is created on a Microsoft Windows machine.

You can enter a nice description for the build step, and optionally add two switches `info` and `stacktrace`. The `info` switch is used to print out more information of the build process, which can be useful in case something goes wrong. If the build causes an exception, the `stacktrace` switch prints out the stack trace of this exception. Sometimes you might need more detailed information, in which case you can use the `full-stacktrace` switch instead.

To finalize the configuration, specify the Gradle tasks you want to execute.
First, execute the `clean` task, to make sure there is no output left from any
previous builds. Second, execute the `build` task, which triggers a build of
all variants. The Jenkins configuration should look like this:

Once you have saved the project configuration, you can run the build.

If your build server is installed on a 64-bit Linux machine, you might run into this exception `java.io.IOException: Cannot run program "aapt": error=2, No such file or directory`. This is because AAPT is a 32 bit application and needs some extra libraries in order to run on a 64 bit machine. To install the necessary libraries, use this command:

```
$ sudo apt-get install lib32stdc++6 lib32z1
```

If the build finishes without any issues, it creates APKs for all your build variants. You can use specific Gradle tasks to distribute these APKs. We will mention automatic distribution at the end of the chapter, as it is not specific to any build system.

TeamCity

Unlike Jenkins, TeamCity is a proprietary product that is free to use only for open source projects. It is created and managed by JetBrains. This is the same company that also created IntelliJ IDEA, which is the IDE that Android Studio is based on. TeamCity supports Android builds with Gradle out of the box.

Setting up TeamCity

If you do not have a running TeamCity installation yet, download it from the JetBrains website (`https://www.jetbrains.com/teamcity`) and follow the steps.

To get started with building Android apps and libraries with TeamCity, you need to make sure the JDK, the Android SDK, and the Android build tools are installed on your build server. You can find the instructions for this in the *Jenkins* section. You also need to add `ANDROID_HOME` to the environment variables of the machine, and point it to the Android SDK directory.

Unlike Jenkins, TeamCity does not require any plugins to trigger Gradle builds, as TeamCity has built-in support for running Gradle.

Configuring the build

To set up an Android build, you start by creating a new project. All you need to provide is a name. Once the project is created, you can start configuring it. First, you need to add a VCS root so that TeamCity can find the source code for your project. Then you need to create a new build configuration. You also need to attach the VCS root to the build configuration. When that is set up, you can add a new build step. If you press the **Auto-detect build steps** button, TeamCity will try to determine the necessary build steps, based on the content of the project. In case of a Gradle-based Android project, the result looks like this:

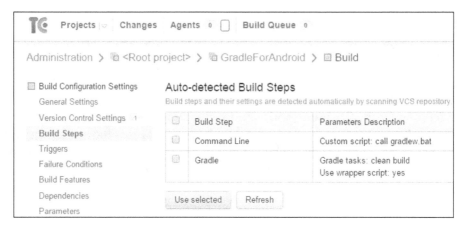

TeamCity detects that the project uses Gradle, and even that the Gradle wrapper is present. You can just select the Gradle build step, and add it to the build configuration. If you do not need to do anything advanced, this is enough to make sure your Android app gets built. You can test the configuration by opening the project overview and clicking on the **Run...** button for the Android project.

Travis CI

If your project's repository is hosted on GitHub, you can use Travis CI for your automated builds. Travis CI (`https://travis-ci.org`) is an open source hosted continuous integration system, and is free to use for public repositories. There is a paid plan for private repositories, but in this book we will only look at the free option.

Travis detects when a new commit is pushed to the repository and starts a new build automatically. By default, Travis builds all branches, not just the master branch. It also builds pull requests automatically; a useful feature for open source projects.

Because of how Travis works internally, you cannot configure the build server itself. Instead, you need to create a configuration file that contains all the information that Travis needs to build your app or library.

Configuring the build

If you want to enable Travis builds for your project, you first need to log in to Travis CI and connect your account to GitHub. Once that is done, you need to enable the project you want to build in the settings.

In order to configure the build process, Travis requires you to create a file called `.travis.yml` that contains the entire setup. To configure an Android project, you need to define the language and add a few Android-specific properties:

```
language: android
android:
  components:
    # The build tools version used by your project
    - build-tools-22.0.1

    # The SDK version used to compile your project
    - android-22

    # Additional components
    - extra-android-m2repository
```

The language setting specifies which kind of build process you want to run. In this case, you are building an Android app. The Android-specific properties include the version of the build tools and the Android SDK version that need to be used. Travis will download those prior to running the `build` tasks. If you make use of the support library or Google Play Services, you need to specify that explicitly because Travis needs to download the repositories for those dependencies as well.

It is not mandatory to configure the build tools and SDK version, but you will encounter fewer issues if you make sure the version aligns with what you have specified in the `build.gradle` file.

If you create an Android project on Microsoft Windows, the Gradle Wrapper file is known to have issues with permissions. Therefore, it is a good idea to fix the permission before running the actual build script. You can add a prebuild step like this:

```
before_script:
  # Change Gradle wrapper permissions
  - chmod +x gradlew
```

To start the build itself, add this line to the Travis configuration file:

```
# Let's build
script: ./gradlew clean build
```

This command will run the Gradle Wrapper, just like you would on a developer machine, and execute the `clean` and `build` tasks.

When you are done configuring the Travis build, you can commit and push the file to the project's GitHub repository. If everything is set up correctly, Travis will start the build process, which you can follow on the Travis website. This is what it looks like when a project is successfully built:

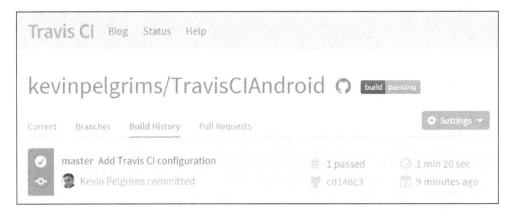

Travis also sends an e-mail report after every build. This can be especially useful if you are the maintainer of an open source library that regularly gets pull requests. The report e-mail from Travis looks like this when a build is successful:

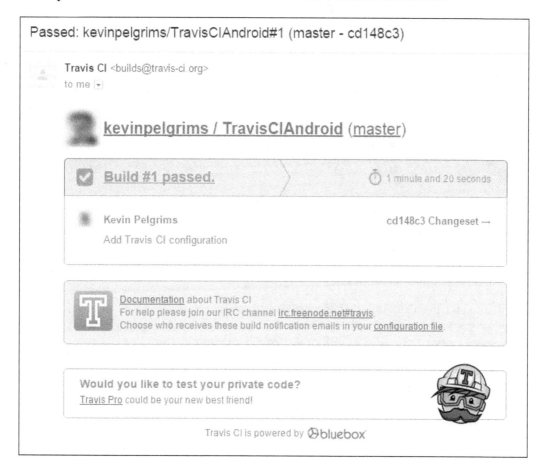

You will quickly notice that Travis has a big downside, and that is speed. Travis does not give you one specific machine, but boots up a vanilla virtual machine for every build you trigger. This means for every new build, Travis has to download and install the Android SDK and build tools, before it can start building your app or library.

On the upside, Travis is free and public, which makes it perfect for open source projects. Travis also builds pull requests automatically, which can give you peace of mind when someone submits a patch to your code.

Further automation

Most modern continuous integration systems support Gradle, either by default or through a plugin. This means that instead of just building your app or library, you can create all kinds of Gradle tasks to further automate the build. The advantage of defining extra build steps with Gradle tasks, instead of in the CI system itself is that the extra build steps become much more portable. It is easy to run a custom Gradle task on your development machine. A custom Jenkins build step, on the other hand, is impossible to run without having Jenkins installed. Having extra build steps in a certain CI system also makes it harder to switch to a different CI system. Gradle tasks can also easily be ported to different projects. In this section, we will look at a few ways to further automate building and deploying apps and libraries, using Gradle tasks and plugins.

The SDK manager plugin

An issue you might run into at some point is that the Android SDK on the build server is not up to date. When you update the SDK version for your app or library, you also need to install the new SDK on the build server. If you have multiple build agents, this becomes a real hassle.

Thanks to community efforts, there is a Gradle plugin that takes care of checking whether the build depends on an Android SDK version that is not present. If the SDK is not present, the plugin will download it automatically.

The SDK manager plugin will download not only the compilation SDK specified in the build configuration file, but also the correct version of the build tools and platform tools. If your project has a dependency on the support library or Google Play Services, the plugin will download the specified version of those as well.

The SDK manager plugin is an open source plugin, you can find the source code for it on GitHub (`https://github.com/JakeWharton/sdk-manager-plugin`).

Running tests

If you want to run unit tests (JUnit or Robolectric) during the build process on the build server, you simply need to add the corresponding tasks to the Gradle execution. If you want to run any functional tests, you will need an emulator to install your app on, so you can run the tests with `gradlew connectedAndroidTest`.

The simplest option for running an emulator is to just launch an emulator on the build server, and keep it open all the time. Unfortunately, this is not an optimal solution, because the Android emulators are quite prone to random crashes, especially when you keep them open for multiple days.

If you are using Jenkins, there is a plugin called **Android Emulator Plugin** (`https://wiki.jenkins-ci.org/display/JENKINS/Android+Emulator+Plugin`) that can be configured to launch an emulator for every build of your app or library. TeamCity also has a lively plugin ecosystem, and there is a plugin called **Android Emulator** that helps setting up an emulator in the same way as the Jenkins plugin. You can find it, along with other TeamCity plugins, on the official TeamCity plugins page (`https://confluence.jetbrains.com/display/TW/TeamCity+Plugins`).

Travis CI has the ability to start an emulator, but this is an experimental functionality. If you want to try it anyway, add this snippet to your `.travis.yml` configuration file to launch an Android emulator during your Travis builds:

```
# Emulator Management: Create, Start and Wait
before_script:
  - echo no | android create avd --force -n test -t android-22 --
    abi armeabi-v7a
  - emulator -avd test -no-skin -no-audio -no-window &
  - android-wait-for-emulator
  - adb shell input keyevent 82 &
```

The `android-wait-for-emulator` instruction tells Travis to wait for the emulator to start. When the emulator is booted, `adb shell input keyevent 82 &` is executed to unlock the screen. After that, you can just tell Gradle to run the tests.

Continuous deployment

To help developers with automatic deployment of Android apps, Google released the Google Play Developer API, an API for pushing APKs to Google Play programmatically (`https://developers.google.com/android-publisher`). This API removes the need for you to open a browser, log in to Google Play, and upload APKs using the web interface. Instead of creating your own publishing script based on the Google Play Developer API, you can use one of the many plugins to push APKs to Google Play directly after a successful build, straight from the build system.

There is a Jenkins plugin called **Google Play Android Publisher** (`https://wiki.jenkins-ci.org/display/JENKINS/Google+Play+Android+Publisher+Plugin`) that can handle this for you. A better option, though, is to use a Gradle plugin, so that you can execute the publishing task from any device and any kind of continuous integration system. Some people in the Android community created a Gradle plugin built around the Google Play Developer API that enables you to configure the entire publishing process. You can find the Gradle Play Publisher Gradle plugin source code on GitHub (`https://github.com/Triple-T/gradle-play-publisher`). It is also available through Maven Central or JCenter.

To start using this plugin, add this to your main `build.gradle` file:

```
buildscript {
    repositories {
        jcenter()
    }

    dependencies {
        classpath 'com.github.triplet.gradle:play-publisher:1.0.4'
    }
}
```

Then apply the plugin in your Android module's `build.gradle` file:

```
apply plugin: 'play'
```

When you apply the Gradle Play Publisher plugin to your build, you will have a few new tasks to your availability:

- `publishApkRelease` uploads the APK and the recent changes
- `publishListingRelease` uploads the descriptions and images
- `publishRelease` uploads everything

If you have different build variants, you can also execute a variant-specific version of these tasks, for example, `publishApkFreeRelease` and `publishApkPaidRelease`.

To get access to the Google Play Developer API, you need to set up a service account. This setup is out of the scope of this book, but it is required if you want to use the Gradle Play Publisher plugin. To get started, follow the steps in the documentation for the Google Play Developer API at `https://developers.google.com/android-publisher/getting_started`.

Once you have created a service account, you can enter the credentials in your build configuration file like this:

```
play {
    serviceAccountEmail = 'serviceaccount'
    pk12File = file('key.p12')
}
```

The `play` block is for properties that are specific for the Gradle Play Publisher plugin. In addition to the service account credentials, you can also specify the track the APK should push to:

```
play {
    track = 'production'
}
```

The default track is `alpha`, but you can change it to `beta` or `production` instead.

Beta distribution

There are a lot of options for beta testing of Android apps, such as the beta track on the Google Play store itself. Another option is **Crashlytics** (`https://crashlytics.com`), which has a very nice integration with Gradle. The team at Crashlytics created a custom plugin that not only creates new Gradle tasks to publish builds to their platform, but also hooks into the Android plugin's tasks to handle ProGuard mapping.

To get started with Crashlytics, follow the steps on their website. Once you have set it up, it will start hooking into your builds. The Crashlytics plugin exposes a new task called `crashlyticsUploadDistributionInternal` that can be used to upload APKs to Crashlytics. To push a new version of your app, you first need to build it using the `build` or `assemble` tasks. Once the APK is ready, you can upload it to Crashlytics using the `crashlyticsUploadDistributionInternal` task. The Crashlytics plugin creates an upload task for every build variant in your project.

Thanks to the custom Gradle plugin, it is very easy for developers to get started with Crashlytics. It also makes it a breeze to upload your test builds to Crashlytics, because you just need to execute one extra task during the build process. This is a great example of how powerful the proper use of Gradle can be, and how a good Gradle plugin can make developers' lives a lot easier.

Summary

In this chapter, we introduced a few popular continuous integration systems, and explained how we can use them to automate building Android apps and libraries. You learned how to configure the CI systems to build Android projects using Gradle. Then we looked at several Gradle plugins to help us further automate the build and deployment processes, and we explained how to run tests automatically on the build server.

In the next chapter, we will look at some more advanced features of Gradle and optimizations for Gradle-based builds. We will also see how we can migrate a big Ant build configuration by using Ant tasks directly from Gradle, and porting them to Gradle in small steps.

9
Advanced Build Customization

Now that you know how Gradle works, how to create your own tasks and plugins, how to run tests, and how to set up continuous integration, you can almost call yourself a Gradle expert. This chapter contains a few tips and tricks that we have not mentioned in the previous chapters that make it easier to build, develop, and deploy Android projects using Gradle.

In this chapter, we will cover the following topics:

- Reducing the APK file size
- Speeding up builds
- Ignoring Lint
- Using Ant from Gradle
- Advanced app deployment

We will start out by looking at how we can reduce the size of the build output and why that is useful.

Reducing the APK file size

The size of APK files has been increasing dramatically in the last few years. There are several causes for this—more libraries have become available to Android developers, more densities have been added, and apps are getting more functionality in general.

It is a good idea to keep APKs as small as possible. Not only because there is a 50 MB limit on APK files in Google Play, but a smaller APK also means that users can download and install an app faster, and it keeps the memory footprint down.

In this section, we will look at a few properties in the Gradle build configuration file that we can manipulate to shrink APK files.

ProGuard

ProGuard is a Java tool that can not only shrink, but also optimize, obfuscate, and preverify your code at compile time. It goes through all the code paths in your app to find code that is not used and deletes it. ProGuard also renames your classes and fields. This process keeps the footprint of the app down, and makes the code more difficult to reverse engineer.

The Android plugin for Gradle has a Boolean property called `minifyEnabled` on the build type that you need to set to true to enable ProGuard:

```
android {
    buildTypes {
        release {
            minifyEnabled true
            proguardFiles getDefaultProguardFile
                ('proguard-android.txt'), 'proguard-rules.pro'
        }
    }
}
```

When you set `minifyEnabled` to `true`, the `proguardRelease` task is executed and invokes ProGuard during the build process.

It is a good idea to retest your entire application after enabling ProGuard, because it might remove some code that you still need. This is an issue that has made lots of developers weary of ProGuard. To solve this problem, you can define ProGuard rules to exclude certain classes from getting removed or obfuscated. The `proguardFiles` property is used to define the files that contain ProGuard rules. For example, to keep a class, you can add a simple rule like this:

```
-keep public class <MyClass>
```

The `getDefaultProguardFile('proguard-android.txt')` method fetches the default ProGuard settings from a file called `proguard-android.txt`, which comes with the Android SDK in the `tools/proguard` folder. The `proguard-rules.pro` file gets added to new Android modules by default by Android Studio, so you can simply add rules specific to the module in that file.

The ProGuard rules are different for each app or library you build, so we will not go into too much detail in this book. If you want to know more about ProGuard and ProGuard rules, check the official Android ProGuard documentation at `http://developer.android.com/tools/help/proguard.html`.

Besides shrinking the Java code, it is also a good idea to shrink the used resources.

Shrinking resources

Gradle and the Android plugin for Gradle can get rid of all unused resources at build time, when the app is being packaged. This can be useful if you have old resources that you forgot to remove. Another use case is when you import a library that has lots of resources, but you only use a small subset of them. You can fix this by enabling resource shrinking. There are two ways to go about shrinking resources, automatic or manual.

Automatic shrinking

The easiest way is to configure the `shrinkResources` property on your build. If you set this property to `true`, the Android build tools will automatically try to determine which resources are not used, and not include them in the APK.

There is one requirement for using this feature, though you have to enable ProGuard as well. This is due to the way the resource shrinking works, as the Android build tools cannot figure out which resources are unused until the code that references these resources has been removed.

The following snippet shows how to configure automatic resource shrinking on a certain build type:

```
android {
    buildTypes {
    release {
            minifyEnabled = true
            shrinkResources = true
        }
    }
}
```

If you want to see exactly how much smaller your APK becomes after enabling automatic resource shrinking, you can run the `shrinkReleaseResources` task. This task prints out how much it has reduced the package in size:

```
:app:shrinkReleaseResources
Removed unused resources: Binary resource data reduced from 433KB
to 354KB: Removed 18%
```

You can get a detailed overview of the resources that are stripped from the APK, by adding the `--info` flag to your build command:

```
$ gradlew clean assembleRelease --info
```

When you use this flag, Gradle prints out a lot of extra information about the build process, including every resource it does not include in the final build output.

One problem with automatic resource shrinking is that it might remove too many resources. Especially resources that are used dynamically might be accidentally stripped out. To prevent this, you can define exceptions in a file called `keep.xml` that you place in `res/raw/`. A simple `keep.xml` file will look like this:

```
<?xml version="1.0" encoding="utf-8"?>
<resources xmlns:tools="http://schemas.android.com/tools"
    tools:keep="@layout/keep_me,@layout/also_used_*"/>
```

The `keep.xml` file itself will also be stripped out of the final result.

Manual shrinking

A less drastic way to strip out resources is to get rid of certain language files or images for certain densities. Some libraries, such as Google Play Services, include a lot of languages. If your app only supports one or two languages, it does not make sense to include all the language files from these libraries in the final APK. You can use the `resConfigs` property to configure the resources you want to keep, and then the rest will be thrown out.

If you want to keep only English, Danish, and Dutch strings, you can use `resConfigs` like this:

```
android {
    defaultConfig {
        resConfigs "en", "da", "nl"
    }
}
```

You can do this for density buckets as well, like this:

```
android {
    defaultConfig {
        resConfigs "hdpi", "xhdpi", "xxhdpi", "xxxhdpi"
    }
}
```

It is even possible to combine languages and densities. In fact, every type of resource can be restricted using this property.

If you are having a hard time setting up ProGuard, or you just want to get rid of resources for languages or densities your app does not support, then using `resConfigs` is a good way to get started with resource shrinking.

Speeding up builds

A lot of Android developers that start using Gradle complain about the prolonged compilation time. Builds can take longer than they do with Ant, because Gradle has three phases in the build lifecycle that it goes through every time you execute a task. This makes the whole process very configurable, but also quite slow. Luckily, there are several ways to speed up Gradle builds.

Gradle properties

One way to tweak the speed of a Gradle build is to change some of the default settings. We already mentioned in parallel build execution in *Chapter 5*, *Managing Multimodule Builds*, but there are a few more settings that you can adjust.

Just to recap, you can enable parallel builds by setting a property in a `gradle. properties` file that is placed in the root of a project. All you need to do is add the following line:

```
org.gradle.parallel=true
```

Another easy win is to enable the Gradle daemon, which starts a background process when you run a build the first time. Any subsequent builds will then reuse that background process, thus cutting out the startup cost. The process is kept alive as long as you use Gradle, and is terminated after three hours of idle time. Using the daemon is particularly useful when you use Gradle several times in a short time span. You can enable the daemon in the `gradle.properties` file like this:

```
org.gradle.daemon=true
```

In Android Studio, the Gradle daemon is enabled by default. This means that after the first build from inside the IDE, the next builds are a bit faster. If you build from the command-line interface; however, the Gradle daemon is disabled, unless you enable it in the properties.

To speed up the compilation itself, you can tweak parameters on the Java Virtual Machine (JVM). There is a Gradle property called jvmargs that enables you to set different values for the memory allocation pool for the JVM. The two parameters that have a direct influence on your build speed are Xms and Xmx. The Xms parameter is used to set the initial amount of memory to be used, while the Xmx parameter is used to set a maximum. You can manually set these values in the gradle.properties file like this:

```
org.gradle.jvmargs=-Xms256m -Xmx1024m
```

You need to set the desired amount and a unit, which can be k for kilobytes, m for megabytes, and g for gigabytes. By default, the maximum memory allocation (Xmx) is set to 256 MB, and the starting memory allocation (Xms) is not set at all. The optimal settings depend on the capabilities of your computer.

The last property you can configure to influence build speed is org.gradle. configureondemand. This property is particularly useful if you have complex projects with several modules, as it tries to limit the time spent in the configuration phase, by skipping modules that are not required for the task that is being executed. If you set this property to true, Gradle will try to figure out which modules have configuration changes and which ones do not, before it runs the configuration phase. This is a feature that will not be very useful if you only have an Android app and a library in your project. If you have a lot of modules that are loosely coupled, though, this feature can save you a lot of build time.

System-wide Gradle properties

If you want to apply these properties system-wide to all your Gradle-based projects, you can create a gradle.properties file in the .gradle folder in your home directory. On Microsoft Windows, the full path to this directory is %UserProfile%\.gradle, on Linux and Mac OS X it is ~/.gradle. It is a good practice to set these properties in your home directory, rather than on the project level. The reason for this is that you usually want to keep memory consumption down on build servers, and the build time is of less importance.

Android Studio

The Gradle properties you can change to speed up the compilation process are also configurable in the Android Studio settings. To find the compiler settings, open the **Settings** dialog, and then navigate to **Build, Execution, Deployment | Compiler**. On that screen, you can find settings for parallel builds, JVM options, configure on demand, and so on. These settings only show up for Gradle-based Android modules. Have a look at the following screenshot:

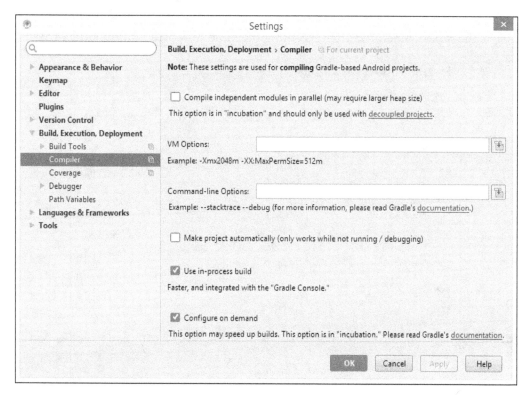

Configuring these settings from Android Studio is easier than configuring them manually in the build configuration file, and the settings dialog makes it easy to find properties that influence the build process.

Profiling

If you want to find out which parts of the build are slowing the process down, you can profile the entire build process. You can do this by adding the `--profile` flag whenever you execute a Gradle task. When you provide this flag, Gradle creates a profiling report, which can tell you which parts of the build process are the most time consuming. Once you know where the bottlenecks are, you can make the necessary changes. The report is saved as an HTML file in your module in `build/reports/profile`.

This is the report generated after executing the build task on a multimodule project:

Profile report

Profiled build: build

| Summary | Configuration | Dependency Resolution | Task Execution |

Summary

Description	Duration
Total Build Time	1m19.46s
Startup	0.867s
Settings and BuildSrc	0.323s
Loading Projects	0.094s
Configuring Projects	2.192s
Task Execution	3m22.12s

Configuration

Project	Duration
All projects	2.192s
:backend	0.879s
:androidlib	0.657s
:	0.486s
:mobile	0.088s
:wear	0.048s
:javalib	0.034s

The profiling report shows an overview of the time spent in each phase while executing the task. Below that summary is an overview of how much time Gradle spent on the configuration phase for each module. There are two more sections in the report that are not shown in the screenshot. The **Dependency Resolution** section shows how long it took to resolve dependencies, per module. Lastly, the **Task Execution** section contains an extremely detailed task execution overview. This overview has the timing for every single task, ordered by execution time from high to low.

Jack and Jill

If you are willing to use experimental tools, you can enable Jack and Jill to speed up builds. **Jack (Java Android Compiler Kit)** is a new Android build toolchain that compiles Java source code directly to the Android Dalvik executable (dex) format. It has its own .jack library format and takes care of packaging and shrinking as well. **Jill (Jack Intermediate Library Linker)** is a tool that can convert .aar and .jar files to .jack libraries. These tools are still quite experimental, but they were made to improve build times and to simplify the Android build process. It is not recommended to start using Jack and Jill for production versions of your projects, but they are made available so that you can try them out.

To be able to use Jack and Jill, you need to use build tools version 21.1.1 or higher, and the Android plugin for Gradle version 1.0.0 or higher. Enabling Jack and Jill is as easy as setting one property in the `defaultConfig` block:

```
android {
    buildToolsRevision '22.0.1'
    defaultConfig {
      useJack = true
    }
}
```

You can also enable Jack and Jill on a certain build type or product flavor. This way, you can continue using the regular build toolchain, and have an experimental build on the side:

```
android {
    productFlavors {
        regular {
            useJack = false
        }

        experimental {
            useJack = true
        }
    }
}
```

As soon as you set `useJack` to `true`, minification and obfuscation will not go through ProGuard anymore, but you can still use the ProGuard rules syntax to specify certain rules and exceptions. Use the same `proguardFiles` method that we mentioned before, when talking about ProGuard.

Ignoring Lint

When you execute a release build with Gradle, a Lint check will be performed on your code. Lint is a static code analysis tool that flags potential bugs in your layouts and Java code. In some cases, it might even block the build process. If you have not used Lint on your project before, and you want to migrate to Gradle, Lint might come up with a lot of errors. To at least make the build work, you can configure Gradle to ignore Lint errors and prevent them from aborting the build, by disabling abortOnError. This should only be a temporary solution, because ignoring Lint errors can result in issues like missing translations, which can cause the app to crash. To prevent Lint from blocking the build process, disable abortOnError like this:

```
android {
    lintOptions {
        abortOnError false
    }
}
```

Temporarily disabling the Lint abort can make it easier to migrate an existing Ant build process to Gradle. Another way to make the transition smoother is to execute Ant tasks directly from Gradle.

Using Ant from Gradle

If you have invested a lot of time in setting up a build with Ant, the switch to Gradle might sound scary. In that case, Gradle cannot only execute Ant tasks, it can also expand them. This means you can migrate from Ant to Gradle in smaller steps, instead of spending several days on converting your entire build configuration.

Gradle uses Groovy's **AntBuilder** for the Ant integration. The AntBuilder enables you to execute any standard Ant task, your own custom Ant tasks, and entire Ant builds. It also makes it possible to define Ant properties in your Gradle build configuration.

Running Ant tasks from Gradle

Running a standard Ant task from Gradle is straightforward. You just need to prepend the task name with ant. and everything works out of the box. For example, to create an archive, you can use this task:

```
task archive << {
    ant.echo 'Ant is archiving...'
    ant.zip(destfile: 'archive.zip') {
        fileset(dir: 'zipme')
    }
}
```

The task is defined in Gradle, but makes use of two Ant tasks, echo and zip.

Of course you should always consider the Gradle alternatives for the standard Ant tasks. To create an archive like in the previous example, you can define a Gradle task that can handle this for you:

```
task gradleArchive(type:Zip) << {
    from 'zipme/'
    archiveName 'grarchive.zip'
}
```

The task for the Gradle-based archive is more concise and easy to understand. Because it does not need to go through the AntBuilder, it is also slightly faster than using the Ant tasks.

Importing an entire Ant script

If you have created an Ant script to build your app, you can import the whole build configuration, using ant.importBuild. All Ant targets are then automatically converted to Gradle tasks that you can access by their original name.

For example, take the following Ant build file:

```
<project>
    <target name="hello">
        <echo>Hello, Ant</echo>
    </target>
</project>
```

You can import this build file into your Gradle build like this:

```
ant.importBuild 'build.xml'
```

This will expose the hello task to your Gradle build, so you can execute it like a regular Gradle task, and it will print out Hello, Ant:

```
$ gradlew hello
:hello
[ant:echo] Hello, Ant
```

Because the Ant task is converted to a Gradle task, you can also extend it using the doFirst and doLast blocks, or the << shortcut. For example, you can print another line to the console:

```
hello << {
    println 'Hello, Ant. It\'s me, Gradle'
}
```

If you execute the `hello` task now, it looks like this:

```
$ gradlew hello
:hello
[ant:echo] Hello, Ant
Hello, Ant. It's me, Gradle
```

You can also depend on tasks imported from Ant, just like you usually would. For example, if you want to create a new task that depends on the hello task, you can simply do this:

```
task hi(dependsOn: hello) << {
    println 'Hi!'
}
```

Using `dependsOn` makes sure the `hello` task gets triggered when executing the hi task:

```
$ gradlew intro
:hello
[ant:echo] Hello, Ant
Hello, Ant. It's me, Gradle
:hi
Hi!
```

If you need to, you can even make an Ant task depend on a Gradle task. To accomplish this, you need to add the `depends` attribute to the task in the `build.xml` file, like this:

```
<target name="hi" depends="intro">
    <echo>Hi</echo>
</target>
```

If you have a big Ant build file, and you want to make sure none of the task names overlap, you can rename all the Ant tasks on import, using this code snippet:

```
ant.importBuild('build.xml') { antTargetName ->
    'ant-' + antTargetName
}
```

If you decide to rename all the Ant tasks, keep in mind that if you have an Ant task that depends on a Gradle task, then that Gradle task needs to be prefixed as well. Otherwise, Gradle will not be able to find it and throw an `UnknownTaskException`.

Properties

Gradle and Ant cannot only share tasks, but you can also define properties in Gradle that can be used in your Ant build files. Consider this Ant target, which prints out a property called `version`:

```
<target name="appVersion">
    <echo>${version}</echo>
</target>
```

You can define the version property in the Gradle build configuration by prepending the property name with `ant.`, just like with tasks. This is the shortest way to define an Ant property:

```
ant.version = '1.0'
```

Groovy hides a lot of the implementation here. If you write the property definition in full, it looks like this:

```
ant.properties['version'] = '1.0'
```

Executing the `version` task will do exactly what you would expect, namely printing out `1.0` to the console:

```
$ gradlew appVersion
:appVersion
[ant:echo] 1.0
```

Having deep Ant integration in Gradle makes it a lot easier to transition from Ant-based builds to Gradle, and you can do it at a pace that you are comfortable with.

Advanced app deployment

In *Chapter 4*, *Creating Build Variants*, we looked at several ways to create multiple versions of the same app, using build types and product flavors. However, in some cases, it might be easier to use a more specific technique, such as APK splits.

Split APK

Build variants can be seen as separate entities, that can each have their own code, resources, and manifest file. APK splits, on the other hand, only impact the packaging of an app. The compilation, shrinking, obfuscation, and so on are still shared. This mechanism allows you to split APKs based on either density or **application binary interface (ABI)**.

You can configure splits by defining a `splits` block inside the `android` configuration block. To configure density splits, create a `density` block inside the `splits` block. If you want to set up ABI splits, use an `abi` block.

If you enable density splits, Gradle creates a separate APK for each density. You can manually exclude certain densities if you do not need them, to speed up the build process. This example shows how to enable density splits and exclude devices with low density:

```
android {
    splits {
        density {
            enable true
            exclude 'ldpi', 'mdpi'
            compatibleScreens 'normal', 'large', 'xlarge'
        }
    }
}
```

If you only support a few densities, you can use `include` to create a whitelist of densities. To use include, you first need to use the `reset()` property, which resets the list of included densities to an empty string.

The `compatibleScreens` property in the preceding snippet is optional, and injects a matching node in the manifest file. The configuration in the example is for an app that supports normal to extra large screens, excluding devices with small screens.

Splitting APKs based on the ABI works in the same way, and all of the properties are the same as the properties for density splits, except for `compatibleScreens`. ABI splits have nothing to do with screen size, so there is no property called `compatibleScreens`.

The result of executing a build after configuring the density splits is that Gradle now creates one universal APK and several density-specific APKs. This means you will end up with a collection of APKs like this:

```
app-hdpi-release.apk
app-universal-release.apk
app-xhdpi-release.apk
app-xxhdpi-release.apk
app-xxxhdpi-release.apk
```

There is one caveat to using APK splits, though. If you want to push multiple APKs to Google Play, you will need to make sure every APK has a different version code. This means that each split should have a unique version code. Luckily, by now you are able to do this in Gradle by looking at the `applicationVariants` property.

The following snippet comes straight from the Android plugin for Gradle documentation, and shows how to generate different version codes for each APK:

```
ext.versionCodes = ['armeabi-v7a':1, mips:2, x86:3]

import com.android.build.OutputFile

android.applicationVariants.all { variant ->
    // assign different version code for each output
    variant.outputs.each { output ->
        output.versionCodeOverride = project.ext.versionCodes.get
            (output.getFilter(OutputFile.ABI)) * 1000000 +
            android.defaultConfig.versionCode
    }
}
```

This little snippet checks which ABI is used on a build variant, and then applies a multiplier to the version code to make sure each variant has a unique version code.

Summary

After reading this chapter, you know how to reduce the size of your build outputs, and how to speed up builds by configuring Gradle and the JVM. Big migration projects should not frighten you anymore. You also learned some tricks that make development and deployment easier.

And with that, you have reached the end of the book! Now that you know the possibilities of Gradle, you can tweak and customize the build processes of your Android projects to the point where you will not need to do any manual work, except for executing tasks. You can configure build variants, manage dependencies, and configure multimodule projects. The Gradle DSL makes sense to you because you understand Groovy syntax, and you are comfortable with hooking into the Android plugin. You can even create tasks or plugins and share them, to help others automate their builds. All you need to do now is to apply your new skills!

Index

Symbol

.aar files
 using 42

A

advanced app deployment
 about 139
 APKs, splitting 139, 140
Android Debug Tool (ADB) 106
Android Developer Tools (ADT) 2
Android Emulator Plugin
 about 123
 URL 123
Android library
 adding, to project 68
Android plugin
 hooking into 104
Android Studio
 about 2, 63
 dependencies, using inside 44, 45
 Gradle tasks, running inside 26, 27
 manifest entries, manipulating inside 29, 30
 module tasks, running from 74
 settings, configuring for speeding
  up builds 133
 update channels 3
Android Studio terminal
 modifying 28
Android tasks 25
Android Virtual Device (AVD) 3
Android Wear
 app, integrating to 69
Ant
 using, from Gradle 136

AntBuilder 136
Ant tasks
 running, from Gradle 136
APK file size
 reducing 127
APKs
 renaming, automatically 104, 105
 splitting 139, 140
app
 integrating, to Android Wear 69
application binary interface (ABI) 139

B

backend
 using, in Google App Engine 72
base tasks
 about 24
 conventions 25
basics, Gradle
 about 3
 build configuration file 4, 5
 build lifecycle 4
 projects 4
 project structure 6
 tasks 4
BuildConfig
 and resources 30, 31
build configuration file 4, 5
build customization
 about 28
 BuildConfig class 30
 default tasks 33
 manifest entries, manipulating 29
 project properties 32
 project-wide settings 31

build lifecycle 4
build process
  profiling 134
builds
  speeding up 131
  speeding up, Gradle properties
      used 131, 132
build types
  about 48
  creating 48, 49
  debug 48
  dependencies 52
  release 48
  source sets 50, 51
  staging 49
build variants
  about 54, 55
  creating 57, 58
  filters 58, 59
  resource and manifest, merging 56
  source sets 56
  tasks 55

C

classes 91
closures 93
collections 93
configurations
  about 42
  androidTestCompile 43
  apk 43
  compile 43
  provided 43
  testCompile 43
continuous integration (CI)
  about 113
  URL 113
Crashlytics
  about 125
  URL 125
credentials
  storing 38
custom plugin
  using 111
custom tasks, Google App Engine 73

D

dependencies
  using, inside Android Studio 44, 45
dependencies, build types 52
dependency management 35
dependency-related concepts
  about 42
  configurations 42
  dynamic versions 44
  semantic versioning 43
Directed Acyclic Graph (DAG) 4
domain-specific language (DSL) 3
dynamic versions 44

E

Eclipse project, to Gradle-based project
  libraries, migrating 18
  manual migration 15-18
  migration 13
  migration, with import wizard 14, 15
entire Ant script
  importing 137, 138
Espresso 82-86
export wizard, Eclipse 15

F

file dependencies 39
filters, build variants 58, 59
functional tests 82
further automation
  about 122
  beta distribution 125
  continuous deployment 123-125
  SDK manager plugin 122
  tests, running 122, 123

G

Google App Engine
  about 70
  backend, using in 72
  build file, analyzing 71, 72
  creating 70, 71
  custom tasks 73

Google Play Android Publisher
  URL 124
Google Play Developer API
  URL 124
Gradle
  about 10
  Ant tasks, running from 136
  Ant, using from 136
  basics 3
  phases 4
  properties, defining in 139
  URL 11
  URL, for installation page 11
Gradle files
  about 19
  module build file 21
  settings file 20
  top-level build file 20, 21
Gradle properties
  used, for speeding up builds 131, 132
Gradle tasks
  running, inside Android Studio 26, 27
Gradle Wrapper
  about 10
  basic build tasks, running 12, 13
  obtaining 10-12
Groovy
  about 3, 89, 90, 94
  URL 90

J

Jack (Java Android Compiler Kit) 135
Jacoco 87
Java library module
  adding, to project 68
Java Virtual Machine (JVM) 3
JDK, from Java website
  URL, for downloading 114
Jenkins
  about 113, 114
  build, configuring 115-117
  setting up 114, 115
  URL 114
Jill (Jack Intermediate Library Linker) 135
JUnit 78- 80

L

library projects
  .aar files, using 42
  about 41
  modules, creating 41
  modules, using 41
Lint
  about 136
  disabling 136
local dependencies
  about 39
  file dependencies 39
  library projects 41
  native libraries 40
local repositories 38

M

manifest entries
  manipulating, inside Android Studio 29, 30
manifest merging
  reference link 57
members 91
methods 92
module build file
  about 21
  android block 22, 23
  dependencies block 24
  plugin 22
module coupling 75
modules
  about 63
  adding, to project 67
module tasks
  running, from Android Studio 74
multiflavor variants, product flavors 53, 54
multimodule build
  anatomy 64, 65
  build lifecycle 65, 66
  module tasks 66
  speeding up 75
multimodule projects
  best practices 73-75
  tips 73-75

N

native libraries 40

P

phases, Gradle
  configuration 4
  execution 4
  initialization 4
plugin, Gradle
  references 110
plugin portal, Gradleware
  URL 110
plugins
  creating 107
  custom plugin, using 111
  distributing 108-110
  simple plugin, creating 107, 108
preconfigured repositories 37
product flavors
  about 52
  creating 52, 53
  multiflavor variants 53, 54
  source sets 53
ProGuard
  about 128
  URL 129
project
  about 4, 63
  creating 7-9
  modules, adding to 67
project structure 6
properties
  defining, in Gradle 139

R

release process
  simplifying, tasks used 100-103
remote repositories 37, 38
repositories
  about 35, 36
  local repositories 38
  preconfigured repositories 37
  remote repositories 37, 38

resource and manifest, build variants
  merging 56
resources
  and BuildConfig 30, 31
  shrinking 129
  shrinking, automatically 129, 130
  shrinking, manually 130
Robolectric 81, 82

S

SDK manager plugin
  about 122
  URL 122
SDK tools, from Android developer website
  URL, for downloading 114
semantic versioning 43
Settings class
  reference link 20
settings file 20
signing configurations
  about 59
  defining 60
  using 61
simple plugin
  creating 107, 108
source sets, build types 50, 51
source sets, build variants 56
source sets, product flavors 53
system-wide Gradle properties 132

T

task names 13
tasks
  about 4, 24, 95
  anatomy 98-100
  Android tasks 25
  assemble 13
  base tasks 24
  build 13
  check 13
  clean 13
  creating, dynamically 105, 106
  defining 95, 97
  used, for simplifying release
      process 100-103

tasks, build variants
  assembleBlue 55
  assembleBlueDebug 56
  assembleDebug 55
TeamCity
  about 113, 117
  build, configuring 118
  setting up 118
  URL 118
TeamCity plugins page
  URL 123
test coverage
  about 86
  enabling 87

top-level build file 20, 21
transitive dependencies 35
Travis CI
  about 113, 119
  build, configuring 119-121
  URL 119

U

unit tests 77
update channels, Android Studio 3

Thank you for buying
Gradle for Android

About Packt Publishing

Packt, pronounced 'packed', published its first book, *Mastering phpMyAdmin for Effective MySQL Management*, in April 2004, and subsequently continued to specialize in publishing highly focused books on specific technologies and solutions.

Our books and publications share the experiences of your fellow IT professionals in adapting and customizing today's systems, applications, and frameworks. Our solution-based books give you the knowledge and power to customize the software and technologies you're using to get the job done. Packt books are more specific and less general than the IT books you have seen in the past. Our unique business model allows us to bring you more focused information, giving you more of what you need to know, and less of what you don't.

Packt is a modern yet unique publishing company that focuses on producing quality, cutting-edge books for communities of developers, administrators, and newbies alike. For more information, please visit our website at www.packtpub.com.

About Packt Open Source

In 2010, Packt launched two new brands, Packt Open Source and Packt Enterprise, in order to continue its focus on specialization. This book is part of the Packt Open Source brand, home to books published on software built around open source licenses, and offering information to anybody from advanced developers to budding web designers. The Open Source brand also runs Packt's Open Source Royalty Scheme, by which Packt gives a royalty to each open source project about whose software a book is sold.

Writing for Packt

We welcome all inquiries from people who are interested in authoring. Book proposals should be sent to author@packtpub.com. If your book idea is still at an early stage and you would like to discuss it first before writing a formal book proposal, then please contact us; one of our commissioning editors will get in touch with you.

We're not just looking for published authors; if you have strong technical skills but no writing experience, our experienced editors can help you develop a writing career, or simply get some additional reward for your expertise.

Android Studio Essentials

ISBN: 978-1-78439-720-3   Paperback: 126 pages

A fast-paced guide to get up and running
with Android application development using
Android Studio

1. Learn to install and configure Android Studio
    on your machine to create your own projects.

2. Test your apps using the Android emulator and
    learn how to manage virtual devices.

3. Familiarize yourself with the fundamentals of
    Android development through an exemplary
    coverage of practical examples, functional code,
    and relevant screenshots.

Effective Gradle Implementation [Video]

ISBN: 978-1-78216-766-2   Duration: 03:07 hours

Build, automate, and deploy your application
using Gradle

1. Setting up basic and multi-module
    Java projects.

2. Learn more about the Gradle JavaScript plugin
    to build your own JavaScript projects.

3. Familiarize yourself with Scala plugin
    support with available tasks, layout, setup,
    and dependencies.

Please check **www.PacktPub.com** for information on our titles

Android Application Development
with Maven

ISBN: 978-1-78398-610-1   Paperback: 192 pages

Learn how to use and configure Maven to support all
phases of the development of an Android application

1. Learn how to effectively use Maven to create,
   test, and release Android applications.

2. Customize Maven using a variety of suggested
   plugins for the most popular Android tools.

3. Discover new ways of accelerating the
   implementation, testing, and maintenance
   using this step-by-step simple tutorial
   approach.

Mastering Apache Maven 3

ISBN: 978-1-78398-386-5   Paperback: 298 pages

Enhance developer productivity and address exact
enterprise build requirements by extending Maven

1. Develop and manage large, complex projects
   with confidence.

2. Extend the default behavior of Maven with
   custom plugins, lifecycles, and archetypes.

3. Explore the internals of Maven to arm yourself
   with knowledge to troubleshoot build issues.

Please check **www.PacktPub.com** for information on our titles

www.ingramcontent.com/pod-product-compliance
Lightning Source LLC
LaVergne TN
LVHW081343050326
832903LV00024B/1295